GROWING

MARIJUANA

FOR BEGINNERS

--

STEP-BY-STEP IN 10 STEPS

OSCAR WHITE

Contents

OSCAR WHITE

GROWING MARIJUANA

FOR BEGINNERS

Introduction

Have you been thinking about growing your own
weed for a long time? Maybe you should start. The
advantages, compared to buying weed on the
street, are many and, moreover, you may find that
it is an experience that can give a lot of
satisfaction.

Deciding to take the plunge and start growing your own cannabis can be a great way to cut costs and finally have control over the quality of what you smoke? Given how many people around the world smoke weed, very few of them make the effort to actually grow it. This means that unless you live in a country that is particularly tolerant of marijuana, such as the Netherlands or Spain, like many, you will have to turn to the black market and drug dealers to meet your needs.The thing is, growing marijuana yourself is really a very simple operation. Of course, there are several techniques, some even very advanced, and there will always be something to learn, but growing at basic levels is quite simple and, once you have read the tips we are about to offer you,

you can easily produce the herb yourself. So, we summarize below the 10 main reasons to grow your own marijuana!

1. SIGNIFICANT MONEY SAVINGS

Weed is expensive when it comes to buying it, but cheap in terms of growing. Depending on the place where you live, the cost per gram can vary, but never in a particularly sensitive way. Of course, there is nothing wrong with supporting the local economy, especially if you have the privilege of living in a place where doing so is legal (or nearly so). However, if you want to save some money, then you just need to start growing. And don't think that to grow weed it is necessary to have a particularly complex, expensive and full of equipment Grow Room. Growing outdoors is also even easier: all you need are seeds, soil, water and light ... and nature will freely do the rest.

2. KNOW WHAT YOU HAVE ON YOUR HANDS

One of the biggest problems buying weed is that you never really know what you are bringing home. Was it sprayed with a large amount of pesticides during cultivation? Has it been infested with parasites? Who knows? Your dealer is unlikely to know, or want to give you an answer. By growing your own weed, you can always keep an eye on the products you are going to use and ultimately the final quality of your buds. And, in addition, you will also have the possibility to dry and cure your marijuana independently. Cannabis curing is the process of breaking down the chlorophyll released from the buds, which greatly improves the quality of your weed and as a result, smoking it will also be a much more enjoyable experience. The fact is, most of the weed out there hasn't been cured as it should, but once you've tried a cured bud you can't go back. Polymerization is the trademark that distinguishes a product of a certain quality, for true connoisseurs.

3. YOU WILL BE SELF-SUFFICIENT

"Drugs allow you to survive times without money, better than money allows you to survive times without drugs." Unless you're lucky enough to live in Amsterdam or Barcelona, you won't be able to choose your favorite buds on a menu, at least not entirely, depending where you live! It is much easier for you to depend on what your friends and friends of your friends have to offer, if you are not forced to hang out with people you would rather avoid. When you become a cultivator, you can escape both bad weed and moments when it is lacking. Not forgetting that you don't even have to make certain nasty suspicious phone calls anymore.

4. A ROOM AVAILABLE TO EXPERIMENT

Growing your own marijuana can mean having a lot of buds to harvest. While buying weed on the street, you have more than once, surely had to ration your stash to avoid running out. It is likely that by cultivating it yourself at some point you will not even know where to put it anymore, since even a single plant can produce huge yields. And that, consequently, implies a certain extra margin to experiment. Why not think about turning the excess crop into something edible (like a Space Cake for example)? Or a dye, easy to dose for more stealthy uses? Perhaps you could spice up your kitchen with some cannabis infused oil. The possibilities are endless and by self-growing your weed you will have enough to explore them all.

5. ESTABLISH A RELATIONSHIP WITH THE PLANT

An added bonus is satisfaction. Knowing that you have grown your buds from seed to finished product with your hands and sweat gives immense satisfaction. All this leads to establishing a deep relationship with your plants, allowing you to truly appreciate the experience and the final result even more. Also, with each cultivation your skill will improve. Growing cannabis is an ongoing learning experience, and knowing that your next result is likely to be better than the last is an exciting prospect. Eventually you may become an expert grower, able to read your plants and find a brilliant solution to improve their quality even while growing. And you will never have to buy marijuana again.

6. MORE VARIETY OF CANNABIS TO CHOOSE FROM

If you have a Cannabis Social Club or a nearby dispensary, you are one of those lucky people who can choose from a menu with several exciting strains. If you don't have that privilege, it means you're either dependent on friends or most of the time on the black market, where you can mostly get a single low-quality variety. Sometimes, more than one variety is offered, but that's not a rule. Self-cultivation gives you many options to choose from. Many indoor growers grow more than one plant. This way, you will have the joy of smoking different cannabis strains with different effects, aromas and flavors. Smoking the same weed every time gets tiring, doesn't it?

7. IT'S FUN TO GROW YOUR OWN MARIJUANA PLANTS

One point that is often overlooked is that growing your own cannabis stash is super fun! It is an extremely exciting hobby and passion because there is so much to learn and experience. Think of all the different varieties, techniques, methods, growing styles and equipment you can experiment with. It is truly gratifying to see the results. Carrying out a new growing method right or growing a delicious strain optimally is sure to put a smile on your face. It's not only fun, but you can also be really proud of yourself!

8. CANNABIS IS EASY TO GROW

Sometimes reading articles on growing cannabis can seem like the hardest thing you can do. However, rest assured, because it is not! Especially when you are using the easy to grow strains and beginner plants, which can be purchased as complete sets. Of course, there are several advanced techniques and growing styles, but you can think about that later. Even a novice can achieve great results with minimal effort. Some tips on easy-to-grow strains to start with might be Northern Lights, Easy Bud, or Critical. These strains are known to be suitable for newbies and for producing large quantities of good buds that will get you excited.

9. THE STIGMA THAT SLINGER AROUND CANNABIS IS FADING

Many people who want to grow their buds hesitate because of the illegality of the plant in their country. And that's right! We don't encourage anyone to break the law, but with the legislation changing in many places, the doors are finally open to buy a box and seeds to get started. Sooner or later legalization, or at least decriminalization, will also come to your country. So, informing yourself and learning how to grow weed in advance is a good start for when it finally becomes legal. There's nothing wrong with doing this, right?

10. YOU WILL HAVE A LOT OF ADDITIONAL VEGETABLE MATERIALS WITH ENDLESS POSSIBILITIES OF USE

As you may already know, it's not just cannabis flowers that can be used, but the whole plant has something to offer. Whether it's the leaves, trimmings, sugar leaves or even branches - they all contain cannabinoids (not the same amount as flowers) and can be used to great effect. Popular uses are: making edibles, tinctures, hash or even to roll a cigar with the leaf. The possibilities are almost endless, see? This way you can increase the benefits of cannabis self-cultivation and get different weed products. You will become a kind of personal dispensary!

Chapter 1 Cannabis

The cannabis plant is also known as ganja or marijuana. Its origins date back to very ancient times, so much so that it is not easy to try to trace the first "use" of its properties back to a precise historical moment. This particular plant species has unique characteristics and is even used as a fiber, but it is evident that marijuana is known and is mainly used for the effects of ganja in terms of psychoactive properties. However, it seems that marijuana was already cultivated over 10,000 years ago, as confirmed by some artifacts that have been found on the island of Taiwan and in other parts of the world, such as caves in the mountains of what is now Romania.

The history of cannabis shows us how marijuana plants over the millennia have found the most disparate uses: personal, medical, commercial and productive. The Chinese for example, as evidenced by several ancient treatises, used it for pharmaceutical purposes, while the Aryans preferred, more simply, to smoke it. Still, the Greeks preferred to use it as a bargaining chip and, therefore, in purely commercial terms, while the main types of ganja were vaporized by the Shiites. Among the other populations that in the course of history have benefited most from the consumption of this commodity, we underline how the Phoenicians used it as a raw material for the construction of sails for their ships and ... the list could go on and on, demonstrating how the history of cannabis and the effects of ganja is much more varied and heterogeneous than one might imagine.

GROWING MARIJUANA

FOR BEGINNERS

The arrival of marijuana in Europe seems to date back to about five hundred years before the birth of Christ, as established by an interesting discovery of an urn in Berlin, containing traces of ganja leaves and seeds. It also seems that its spread was very rapid and soon reached every corner of the old continent. To counter its use and further dissemination, a papal bull of 1484 attempted to prohibit its consumption by the people, but with poor results. In Paris, consuming marijuana became a real pastime for the intellectuals of the time, so much so that a club was founded, called `` the club of hashish eaters ", which included famous literary figures, such as Charles Baudelaire, Alexander Dumas and Victor Hugo. In addition to being smoked by the most famous writers of the period, marijuana offered them an "unsuspected" helping hand: it was also used as an element to produce literary works. Just think of the paper made from hemp, used for printing the Gutenberg Bible and even for the Declaration of Independence of the United States of America. Or, in larger dimensions, to be able to make the same sails of the caravels that Christopher Columbus used for his crossings and to reach America, which was already strewn with entire plantations of this plant.

The marijuana plant belongs to the cannabis family, which includes cannabis and humulus, that is, hops. Some substances with hallucinogenic active ingredients are obtained from the processing of Cannabis, such as marijuana and hashish, and also, the most used fiber in the world, namely hemp. Cannabis is a plant with an annual cycle and looks like a thin, straight stem with many branches. Its height is generally between one and a half and two meters, but in some cases it can even reach five meters. Its roots are very large, deep and very branched. The ganja leaves are connected directly to the stem via the petiole (hence the term " petiolate ") and their webbed or lobed shape can have a variable number of " fingers " or small elements with serrated or toothed margins. The number is on average between five and thirteen elements. They have a decent level of health, so much so that cannabis leaf diseases are quite rare. Cannabis is a dioecious plant, i.e. the organs suitable for reproduction, both male and female, i.e. the stamens and pistils, grow on shrubs of different sex. The stamiferous flowers, that is the male ones, are composed in a sort of small panicles and are located exactly under the " axils " of the leaves. Each of these flowers is composed of five petals fused together at the base, and an equal number of stamens. The pistil-bearing flowers, on the other hand, ie the female ones, are grouped in groups of two to six, in correspondence with the bracts, mutated leaves that form the basis of the flowers and inflorescences, from which they originate as small spikes. Each of these flowers then has a membrane that encloses the ovary in a calyx shape, from which two stems emerge, which are nothing more than the natural extension of the ovary that come out of the calyx itself, and two stigmas, the elements that then they are involved in pollination. Flowering occurs in the summer and pollination occurs through the action of the wind, which is why it is called "anemophilous". Cannabis also produces fruit, which have the typically round or oval shape of alkenes but are very hard. They appear in autumn and only host one seed inside. The color of the fruit varies from olive green to reddish and dark brown.

To the question `` what are the different varieties of Cannabis " there seems to be no precise answer, since a controversy has opened up on the matter that has been going on for many years. As always, in the scientific field, there are groups that oppose each other, and also in this case there is a group of scholars who speak of three different existing species, in front of other strands of scholars who instead claim that the species is only one, even with different varieties. In particular, with regard to the hypothesis of who speaks of a unique species but with different varieties, it may be useful to remember that these statements are based on the fact that every cannabis plant has identical chemical and morphological characteristics, and also their development - basically - it's the same. The differences between the various plants therefore do not derive from a different genetic structure, but from the place where they were cultivated, from their properties and from the quality of the soil in which they were planted, and furthermore from other elements such as altitude, the temperature, the cultivation method and many other factors that can affect the success of the cultivation. However, regardless of what has been discussed on a scientific level, three different cannabis species can be distinguished. Let's find out more about ganja bud and ganja effects in the next few lines.

Cannabis Sativa

Cannabis Sativa is the most widespread and known species. Its origin is varied, as it can come from Asia, Africa and America. This cannabis species, when allowed to grow, is capable of reaching five meters in height. It owes its appearance to a long and continuous process of adaptation to different climatic conditions, especially the wetter ones. Among the various species it is the one with the least compact appearance and the period in which flowering occurs can last for fourteen weeks. The leaves have a light green color, are large and very reminiscent of a hand, with the classic long-limbed extensions.

Cannabis Indica

Cannabis Indica is native to the areas of India and Pakistan, and has a completely different physical structure from the first. Due to the adaptation to the drier climate, in fact, it appears as lower and wider, and the color of the leaves is a dark green. Furthermore, it can be easily recognized by the fact that the leaves themselves are much wider and the flowering forms small clusters.

Cannabis Ruderalis

Cannabis Ruderalis is perhaps the most resistant and adapted to the harshest climates. This cannabis species is in fact native to the areas of Siberia and Kazakhstan, places where the sunlight lasts only a few hours a day and the climates are particularly harsh. The flowering of this plant, therefore, does not depend on exposure to the sun, but on other factors. It comes in the form of a small bush, has a very rapid development and can extend in all directions. The maximum height it can reach is about ninety centimeters. Among the three species, it is the one with the thinnest leaves and its flowering generates very small flowers.

Cannabis and its active ingredients: the effects of ganja

The ganja plant contains about eighty cannabinoids, including CBD - or Cannabidiol and THC - or Tetrahydrocannbinol. The latter is the one most sought after by those who use marijuana, given and considered its effects on the body. There is also another term to indicate THC, delta9 Tetrahydrocannabinol: its greatest concentration is found in the leaves and flowers of the plant.

The greatest psychoactive effects are attributed to THC, and it is these consequences that have resulted in the illegality of cannabis in various countries of the world. However, note that the marijuana plant itself does not contain THC, but a similar, non-psychoactive substance, namely tetrahydrocannabinolic acid, known as THCA. The transformation from THCA to THC takes place during the drying process of the plant, since the heat itself used for drying favors and accelerates the process, acting as a catalyst. When THC enters the body, it binds to nerve cells and receptors, promoting the release of a substance known as dopamine, a neurotransmitter naturally produced in every individual by one's brain, which is none other than the hormone that causes THC euphoria. Depending on the cannabinoid concentration, different effects are recorded starting from half an hour after taking it and in some cases they can last over two hours.

The most common symptoms are disorientation, a sense of relaxation, increased appetite, strong euphoria and altered audio-visual perceptions, as well as altered perception of space and time.

There are many studies that, however, would demonstrate the effectiveness of the use of cannabis also in the medical field, for the treatment of those diseases that afflict patients with severe pain, which thanks to the effects caused by the active ingredients, find relief from their suffering condition.

However, there is no study that confirms the rumor that cannabis is also used to treat cancer or similar diseases, since its effect does not counteract the appearance or development of cancer cells, nor is it able to kill them. Its use in the medical field is therefore limited to its relaxing and pain-relieving effects for the time being.

Different percentages of THC

According to the different cannabis species there are then various percentages of THC. In Sativa, for example, the THC percentage is around one or two percent and, only in some cases, it can be as high as five percent. In some areas of India, however, there are different variants capable of reaching much higher percentages, even around twenty-five percent. Ruderalis, on the other hand, is the one with the lowest percentages. In recent legal cannabis, for example, we recall how the percentage of THC is limited by law to 0.6 percent. As for the non-psycho-active element of Cannabis, CBD, remember that it has a double function on THC: it causes the analgesic effect of THC to last longer and at the same time, counteracts its negative effects. on changes in temperature, increased breathing and changes in heart rate. Among the side effects of taking THC we point out two particularly discussed, such as the feeling of paranoia and anxiety. These effects, however, are not recorded on the intake of CBD, as confirmed by several studies. Therefore, those who consume THC regularly could expose themselves to the risk of showing the clear symptoms of psychosis, so much so that often the therapies to heal from these side effects include the administration of CBD, which counteracts the psychotic effects. Furthermore, THC, when taken in high concentrations, induces a state of wakefulness and counteracts sleep, with a mechanism that is basically the opposite of that of CBD, which instead stimulates sleep.

CBD is a substance that has been identified as a legal solution to THC, giving rise to the so-called cannabis light, which contains very low percentages of THC, always and in any case within 0.6 percent and various concentrations of CBD. This is now legally sold in numerous smoke shops throughout the territory, and can also be legally purchased online.

What is legal or light cannabis

When we talk about legal or light cannabis, we are talking about the product of the female flowers of Cannabis Sativa.

In fact, remember that these are the elements of the plant that contain the lowest percentage of THC, starting from 0.2 percent and by law, allowed up to 0.6 percent. However, these parts of cannabis contain high amounts of CBD.

Due to these characteristics, the female inflorescence of Cannabis Sativa is not to be considered as a narcotic substance and which due to its low levels of Tetrahydrocannabinol differs from classic marijuana, which can be found for therapeutic reasons, but used for illegal purposes.

The appearance is the same as that of classic marijuana and only through a chemical analysis could the legal from the illegal one be distinguished. For this reason, drug dealers sell cannabis light as hashish or marijuana.

The benefits and properties of Cannabis light

First of all it is good to know that, according to the law, Cannabis, to be defined light, must meet the following criteria:

- the percentage of THC must be between 0.2 and 0.6 percent, tolerance included;
- the percentage of CBD must be less than four percent.

Furthermore, it must be obtained, as already mentioned, from Cannabis Sativa, which over the years has been the subject of many botanical studies and many scientific experiments, aimed at finding a product without any effect from a psychic point of view.

The effects of legal marijuana containing a high rate of cannabidiol are mainly anti-epileptics, muscle relaxants, antioxidants and anti-inflammatories. It induces a feeling of tranquility noticeable by the person, due to the THC content it contains, even if this is practically negligible.

Precisely for this reason, cannabis light does not cause the same effects as classic marijuana, such as potential anxiety, paranoia, euphoria or other psychotropic effects, especially in the case of prolonged and regular use.

The high concentrations of CBD also make Cannabis light a valid ally against migraines, menstrual pain and problems on joints, while the low THC rate induces a state of wakefulness, thus keeping the subject alert.

Obviously, the topic of light cannabis is not always devoid of reflex aspects, and according to some experts it would be advisable not to underestimate some, such as the link between the substance, the methods of intake and the characteristics of the organism of each consumer, despite the cannabinoids present in the plant are in carboxylated form, that is not active, and for this very reason, they cannot cause any psychoactive effect on the nervous system. This is because, very often cannabis is `` turned on " and the heating or lighting of the substance is a process that involves the activation of the active ingredients of the cannabinoids (which is why the consumption by aspiration of the fumes of Cannabis light, is illegal).

For this reason, when you want to use Cannabis light, it is good to carefully evaluate the amount of THC present in marijuana, so as not to suffer the psychoactive effects and not to induce the same responses in the brain from illegal marijuana.

Generally, however, if legal cannabis is smoked, the effects are felt after a few minutes and tend to last up to four hours. In case of ingestion, for example through infusions or decoctions, the reaction times are a little longer than the first, but as regards the duration of these, they can be felt up to fourteen hours.

Contraindications and damage caused by Cannabis light

Cannabis light, thanks to its composition, does not in itself present any contraindications, does not involve any risk and no side effects have been recorded so far. The only problems deriving from light marijuana, not to be underestimated, are those resulting from combustion, even comparable to those caused by classic cigarettes, such as malignant neoplasms, damage to the respiratory and cardio-vascular systems, etc.

As for the use of cananbis light on pregnant women, this use is clearly not recommended, as it seems to have potentially negative effects on the placenta and its protective functions. Another problem indirectly deriving from cannabis light is the consumption of this in association with normal tobacco, since, precisely this mix, can cause a type of addiction in the subject, known as smoking.

In addition, special attention must be paid to driving vehicles after consuming cannabis light. This in fact, even if it has no psycho-active effects and therefore does not affect the driving skills, however, as it contains a certain percentage of THC, it can be detected in a possible control, making the subject positive to the test who is therefore declared not able to drive , with all the due consequences provided for by law.

Finally, in case the subject is suffering from respiratory or cardiac disorders, the intake of cannabis light is not recommended.

Finally, we conclude with the invitation to make an important distinction between the different legal and non-legal substances, and how it is therefore necessary to clarify that the origin of certain drugs is different from that of marijuana, as well as the their effects.

Opiates, for example, originate from opium alkaloids, naturally contained in the resin extracted from poppy flowers, known substances that have the same origin are morphine, codeine and even heroin, as well as the so-called opioids, i.e. products synthesized in the laboratory by the processing of opium.

Hallucinogens, on the other hand, are synthetic drugs that cause hallucinations, also called psychedelic drugs, of which, for example, the so-called `` magic mushrooms " and the well-known LSD belong. These release serotonergic agents, clouding the subject's mind. These substances, once in the body, bind to the receptors of serotonin, a neurotransmitter that has the task of sending signals to the brain, in some cases favoring and in others disfavouring the impulses sent to the brain.

Cannabis is better!

That said, it is easy to understand why cannabis, whether it is classic or light, is different from the substances just mentioned. First of all, its origin is absolutely natural and even in the case of natural opiate substances, the same effects in nature are very different. Cannabis also undergoes a simple drying process, like tobacco, which simply serves to maintain the freshness of the leaves and leaves the active ingredients intact, without altering them. Opiate substances, on the other hand, undergo chemical processes, are heavily treated in the laboratory, and the refining or cutting processes often take place through substances that are highly harmful to the body and the nervous system, while the psychoactive effects of these substances are much more dangerous, both for the organism and health of the subject, and for the behavior towards third parties that this can assume. The same goes for hallucinogens, which are now mainly chemical products. The psycho-active effects of cannabis, while affecting perception, are ultimately still relaxing and moreover, absent in cannabis light.

Chapter 2 The Resin

What is the first thing you think about when you hear the word "cannabis"? You probably think of the hemp leaf, with its characteristic serrated shape along with its long, tapered tips. Indeed, the leaf and its inflorescences are the most used part of Cannabis Sativa. But there is something else about the hemp plant that can be used: among the verdant leaves lies a precious treasure, the cannabis resin.

Let's see exactly what it is and what its uses are.

What is cannabis resin?

The resin of Cannabis Sativa is a golden nectar that is secreted by the trichomes to defend against bacteria, parasites, insects and even ultraviolet rays! However, its smell attracts pollinating insects, which are essential for the reproduction of the plant. Resin is found on all cannabis plants, but is produced to a greater extent by unpollinated female plants.

The nectar of these plants is rich in cannabidiol, better known as CBD, which lends itself to various applications.

CBD is an active ingredient contained in Cannabis Sativa with relaxing and anti-inflammatory effects, without any psychoactive effect.

CBD resin

There are various methods for extracting cannabis resin. Some, more coarse, involve the extraction of the active principle by drying the plant using oils or alcohol; but to obtain the purest and highest quality resin supercritical CO2 technology is used. With this sophisticated extraction method, a very pure cannabis resin is obtained, ready to be used in various ways. The extract is amber in color and retains the characteristic smell of cannabis. If it has a greenish hue, it means that it has been roughly extracted and purified. Compared to the more classic cannabis oils, the resin has a very high percentage of CBD.

How is the resin used?

The CBD resin can be used like cannabis oil, bearing in mind that the concentration of the active ingredient is higher and that it has beneficial substances such as polyphenols and terpenes. The amber color and its particular consistency, however, make it different from classic oils. It should be dispensed through the use of a practical dropper: to ensure maximum precision, it is advisable to just press on the syringe plunger, and then take the drop with a toothpick or directly on the finger. The resin drops can be taken directly orally, putting them in contact with the mucous membrane of the mouth. In this way, the intake will be quick and its positive effects will manifest immediately. But it can also be taken through food and drink. The possibilities are endless.

Chapter 3 CBD and THC

The substances contained in cannabis are not all the same. It is therefore good to clarify for all those who want to introduce themselves to this interesting world, full of benefits for health and to live better.

CBD, which stands for cannabidiol, is a substance found in hemp. Its main feature is that it does not possess psychoactive effects or does not modify the psycho-physical state such as attention, perception, consciousness, behavior, does not create addiction and is particularly suitable for the treatment of certain pathologies, so much so that many scientific studies are confirming the validity of this substance also in the field of medicine.

In legal cannabis, the level of THC, the psychotropic substance, is below 0.6% as required by the Laws.

The advantage is that it gives a relaxing effect without creating addiction.

Before knowing the beneficial properties of what is in effect a metabolite, that is the product of the final process of metabolism in the body, it would be appropriate to distinguish between CBD and THC, the main elements of cannabis.

The first is a non-psychoactive cannabinoid that binds to CB2 receptors present in the T cells of the immune system and stimulates healing; the second instead is a psychoactive substance that binds to CB1 receptors, alters the mind and causes euphoria, increased appetite, relaxation and loss of space-time perception.

Precisely the presence of the THC substance within cannabis ensures that the legal status around the world on hemp remains on controversial positions. Science, and therefore the jurisprudence of many states, considers 0.6% to be the maximum limit not to be exceeded and within which they have no psychotropic effects.

In fact, several investigations would testify to the benefits of THC on the treatment of some diseases with percentages above 0.6%, which however must always be administered under medical supervision. For the inflorescences to be smoked with THC below 0.6% we speak of legal cannabis. In this regard, as in fruit trees, and more generally in agriculture, there are different genetic selection techniques, this also applies to the cultivation of hemp, geared precisely to a greater production of CBD.

Hemp has been an ally of man for millennia for the benefits also for the environment but its nature and use have been distorted for mere lobbyist reasons.

CBD: all the benefits for physical and mental health

Cannabidiol has several benefits for physical and mental health. Let's see which are the most important. Thanks to its ability to reduce muscle spasms, it is for example indicated in pathologies that cause convulsions, including epilepsy. The latter pathology in some cases is in fact immune to traditional medicines, so much so that some doctors administer alternative therapy based on cannabidiol, which has antiepileptic, anti- spasmodic and anticonvulsant effects. This substance is also particularly effective in counteracting forms of anxiety and stress, insomnia and depression thanks to its antipsychotic and calming effects. Its use is indicated in particular forms of anxiety such as post traumatic stress disorder and obsessive compulsive disorder.

Important anti-inflammatory properties are also attributed to cannabidiol. Precisely for this reason the substance is often used to fight various skin diseases such as acne and psoriasis. On the epidermis it is extremely functional because the oil obtained from hemp hydrates and softens the skin thanks to the action of essential fatty acids and performs an important anti-aging action that keeps the skin young and elastic with the help of antioxidants.

Its antibacterial properties are known, thanks to which it regenerates tissues and improves the appearance of the hair. It can also be prescribed for neuropathies and fibromyalgia.

Again: several studies have confirmed that cannabidiol is useful in preventing the emergence of neurodegenerative diseases. It can also be an excellent analgesic, since it reduces the sense of nausea, relieves pain, stimulates appetite and improves digestibility.

The relaxing and calming effects of this substance are very effective in reducing tension, inflammation and pain associated with various pathologies, and sometimes cannabis is also used in oncology, to decrease the side effects of chemotherapy. Finally, positive effects were also found in those suffering from arteriosclerosis, arthrosis and diseases of the circulatory system.

A question that is dear to many has to do with the side effects of CBD: does it have any? And if it does, what are they? The answer is clear: before taking this substance it is advisable to consult a trusted doctor for a competent opinion.

For example, one of the main side effects is drowsiness: it is therefore advisable not to drive after taking cannabinol. In case of prolonged administration the maximum recommended dose to be taken is 300 mg, while a larger quantity is indicated only for a short treatment.

In any case, we must not exceed as the abuse of this substance can cause in the most serious cases diarrhea, dry mouth, fatigue, pressure drops and sudden attacks of hunger.

THC, what is tetrahydrocannabinol: recreational and healing purposes

Let's see instead what are the characteristics of THC, which, we have seen, has psychotropic effects. The use of hemp for its psychoactive properties can be motivated for different reasons. One of the purposes is recreational, with the intent of altering the mind to feel more relaxed or to entertain oneself.

In this sense, hemp with THC is considered by experts to be a dissociative substance, which can generate an alienating effect. Although the active ingredient of cannabis (THC) does not cause narcotic consequences, such as heroin or opioids, at the same time, however, it differs from cocaine because it is neither exciting nor euphoric. What, then, does this alienating effect consist of? Quite simply in a dissociation whereby the mind is distracted from itself.

However, it is good to keep in mind that in regular users, what has been called cannabis amotivational syndrome is created, a sort of constant laziness that inhibits one from carrying out projects and being active in life. In short, the use of cannabis can be problematic if it is compulsive and is not carried out with responsibility and medical supervision. Another type of use, quite different, can be to benefit from soothing and healing properties that are precious for those suffering from various ailments, even serious ones.

Treatment of various severe neurological diseases can benefit from using hemp. In general, cannabis provides pain relief, especially for cancer patients, but it is also recommended for those who suffer from chronic conditions that are associated with spinal cord injury or multiple sclerosis.

In addition, it may be recommended to overcome some side effects of HIV-specific therapies, radiotherapy and chemotherapy. Also among cancer patients, it serves to stimulate appetite.

Much research has been published in the US National Library of Medicine National Institutes of Health, the Bible of medical information. This journal is continuously updated by the scientific community because many other effects of cannabinoids are still unknown. In short, the research on these substances still reserves many surprises.

Chapter 4 How Much THC And CBD Our Plants Will Have

How much THC and CBD will your plants have? Is there a limit? Let's take a look inside cannabis plants to see how genetics determine cannabinoid content and find out whether or not the effects of a strain can be predicted according to its THC and CBD values.

When you first venture into the world of cannabis cultivation, there are a few things to keep in mind. Have you set up an appropriate growing environment? Can you keep it under constant control? Do you already know what to do with the plants as soon as they are ready? All of these aspects are important, but perhaps so is the question of cannabinoid content.

How much THC and CBD will my plants have? Once you understand this, you can start making some predictions about the effects you will get. And even before that, you may be intrigued by the factors that influence these values.

How Genetics Influences Relationships Between THC and CBD

During its genetic development, a cannabis plant synthesizes both CBDA and THCA (which turn into CBD and THC when heated) from the same cannabinoid: CBGA. The fact that one, the other or both appear depends on an enzyme that can take one of the two forms, which we will call A and B, encoded by the same gene. Since each plant receives two copies of the gene, there are only three possibilities. The plant has two copies of the gene that codes for A, has one copy of both genes that code for A and B, or has two copies of the gene that codes for B. This distribution determines the amounts of CBDA and THCA present in plants.

Those that contain two copies of the gene that codes for A will end up being strains with strong CBD dominance and minimal THC levels, such as Solomatic CBD. Plants with one copy of each gene will end up having a 1: 1 ratio, such as Painkiller XL and Dance World. Eventually, those with two copies of the gene that codes for B will become strains with a strong THC dominance. Among these we find many genetics that we often hear about today, such as Royal Gorilla.

Because strains have THC and CBD limits

The THC concentrations of modern cannabis plants are higher than ever. However, they tend to always stay below the maximum peak they can reach. This happens because both THC and CBD are derived from the same gene, which means that there are strict limits on the possible ratios of both. For THC, this limit is around 35% by dry weight, but most strains classified as potent reach 25-30%. The upper limit for CBD, on the other hand, is around 20-25%, which we can find in strains such as Solomatic CBD, which contains 21% CBD. If we then consider the strains that contain significant amounts of both cannabinoids, the limits are even more articulated. Therefore, you are unlikely to come across a strain with 30% THC and 10% CBD, and vice versa.

Once you have an idea of the THC and CBD content of your plants, you can start making some assumptions about their possible effects. Most of us are familiar with the effects of THC-dominant strains: increased appetite, decreased energy, sharper senses, laughter, etc. Those with CBD dominance, on the other hand, will not have psychoactive effects, but will cause more sub-perceptual sensations. Strains with balanced concentrations of THC and CBD vary in terms of psychoactivity and are the most popular with many consumers because their effects tend to be more balanced than those of strains with a strong THC dominance.

Thanks to recent advances in the cannabis industry, today there are several methods to check the percentages of THC and CBD. Each of these have their own strengths, but the most popular one is probably high-performance liquid chromatography (HPLC). Used by more than half of the industry, this technique requires no heating and always guarantees accurate and more precise results than other methods. However, there are also other equally good analysis techniques, such as gas chromatography, which can also detect volatile hazardous compounds. As such, it is regularly used to check for solvent residues.

That said, the most accessible method to everyone, which still continues to offer more than satisfactory results today, is thin layer chromatography (TLC). Usually, it consists of a glass or plastic sheet containing a thin layer of silica gel, cellulose or aluminum oxide. A solution containing the cannabis sample is then placed on this "plate", where a solvent is applied which, by capillary action, separates the components of the solution. From that moment, the samples are ready to be analyzed using the appropriate TLC test kits. It sounds like a rather complex process, but in reality it is quite simple to use. These kits can be ordered online on several sites.

Another method is supercritical fluid chromatography. It is a technique that uses CO_2 in the supercritical state, which allows the effectiveness of a liquid and the practicality of a gas. On balance, CO_2 is recycled and potentially hazardous solvents eliminated from the process.

Most dispensaries, coffeeshops and seed banks provide data on their products, informing shoppers of the amounts of THC contained in their buds based on laboratory analysis. After receiving the data from one of the aforementioned outlets, you can use these numbers to put together a quick equation and figure out how much THC or CBD you will be inhaling with each gram of weed.

Let's say you've just grabbed an ounce of your favorite strain while wandering around Amsterdam's coffeeshops. When evaluating your options, the budtender informs you that that particular strain contains around 20% THC.

To get a better idea of how much THC you'll be inhaling with that strain, simply visualize these simple equations in your mind:

1 gram = 1000mg

1 gram of the variety contains 20% THC

20% of 1000mg = 200mg

You can apply the same calculation to CBD concentrations. The high-CBD Solomatic CBD strain contains 21% CBD and approximately 1% THC. Therefore, each gram offers around 10mg of THC and 210mg of CBD.

Of course, other variables also come into play in determining the exact amount of THC / CBD you will consume. For example, let the joint burn in the ashtray while discussing philosophy and botany with your smoker friend? Regardless, the equation above will still give you a general indication of how much THC or CBD you are consuming.

Chapter 5 The Stages Of Cannabis Cultivation

Transforming the cannabis plant from start to finish is a joyful but sometimes difficult process. Like other living things, cannabis plants have specific growth periods. Here we will illustrate each of its periods. Transforming the cannabis plant from start to finish is a beautiful process! Like all living things, marijuana goes through different stages of growth and all of them need attention and care. For example, some phases require precise amounts of light while others require larger quantities of water and specific nutrients. Whether you are interested in growing a plant for yourself or are interested in learning more about how to grow cannabis, it is important to know the ins and outs of each step. There are exactly four crucial stages: germination, seedling, vegetative and flowering. And finally, there is also the collection phase. It is not necessarily part of the plant's life cycle although, nevertheless, it is a key point. And now, let's dive into these phases, what do you say?

THE GERMINATION PHASE

The first step in growing cannabis is the germination phase (1-2 weeks), starting from seed. During this time, the marijuana plant is dormant and needs water to start thriving. The quality of the seed depends on the color and structure. What you need to look for is a dry and hard seed, with a light or dark brown color. What should be avoided is a soft, white or green seed. If you are using that type of seed, nine times out of ten they will fail to germinate. Germination takes about 24 hours to seven days. Once you notice that the seeds have opened, you will know that the plant is ready to grow. As the taproot pushes down, the seedling will grow skyward. At first, two leaves called cotyledons will appear which will be attached to the stem once it comes out of its protective shell.

These leaves are the same leaves that will nourish the plant allowing it to grow safely and healthily. Once the roots have formed, you will notice the main leaves thriving. At that point, you can officially say that your plant is a seedling. During the seedling phase (2-3 weeks, 18-24 hours of light), your plant will develop other leaves, the classic ones of marijuana. At first, it will be a serrated leaf with a single tip.

The more it grows, the more it will put out leaves with multiple tips. Usually, a mature plant will have between 5 and 7 tips per leaf. However, some plants are known to produce multiple spikes. As long as a cannabis plant does not form leaves with a sufficient number of tips, it will be considered a seedling. A healthy seedling will need to be short with strong growth. The leaves should be a bright green color. If the plant stretches towards the sky, it could indicate a problem. It is important to note that this stage attracts mold and disease. So, make sure the air is clean and keep humidity levels in check.

Vegetative phase

The next stage is the vegetative stage (2-8 weeks, 13-24 hours of light). This is the period in which most of the growth occurs. At this point, your plant will need to be moved to a larger pot to allow it to develop quickly. That is the right time to patch and train your plant. The more your plant grows, the more you need to increase the amount of water when watering.

When it is small, your plant needs to be watered near the stem. As it gets bigger and consequently with longer roots, you will need to water your plant away from the stem to allow water to reach the root tips. In case you don't know, vegetative plants love nutrients that come from healthy soils. So, fertilize them the right way by increasing nitrogen levels. When a plant in the vegetative stage approaches the flowering stage, you can determine if it is male or female simply by looking at the pre-flowers that are between the internodes.

With female pre-flowers, you will notice hair that resembles the pistils on the buds. Males, on the other hand, have small pockets that contain pollen. The further a plant advances in the vegetative stage, the easier it is to discover its sex. Keep in mind that it is important to separate males from females to avoid pollination. However, this is an exception when you want to cross plants on purpose.

Flowering Stage

Finally, the flowering phase arrives (6-8 weeks with 12 hours of light). When the plant receives less than 12 hours of light per day and summer days become shorter or the indoor light cycle is shortened, flowering occurs naturally. And then, sweet and resinous buds will grace you with their presence. At this point, there are a few things to look out for. The first is that plants should not be pruned until they are at least two weeks into bloom. Doing so can irritate the plant's hormones. The second thing is to support and fence your plants. By doing this, you can help the plant support the buds that it produces so hard. Last but not least, think about feeding your plants with nutrients for flowering. Go easy on the water, many go too far when growing cannabis. Again, harvesting is not part of your plant's life cycle. However, knowing when to harvest is crucial. It not only determines the flavor of your cannabis but also the aroma, weight and effect - all of which are essential. Like everything related to marijuana, pinpointing the exact time to collect can be tricky. A good tip is to observe your plants in order to notice any small changes. For a more general observation, look at the pistils. If you don't know what they are, they are found in buds and are white hairs that eventually turn brown or red as the grass matures. When the pistils begin to turn brown, it is a good indicator for looking at the trichomes.

Now, to see them on your tops, you will need a pocket microscope. When the sheer trichomes go opaque, the buds will have reached their maximum intensity and you will need to harvest them immediately before it's too late.

Chapter 6 The First Steps

Before you start planting seeds in the ground, think about what type of grower you want to be. Are you running an indoor operation or do you work in large open spaces? Do you have the right equipment for your growing environment? Have you chosen seeds that will thrive in the environment they will be grown in, indoors or outdoors? Speaking of this last point, every aspiring grower should know the difference between photoperiod and autoflowering cannabis plants. There are some key differences to note.

PHOTOPERIOD PLANTS

The main characteristic of a photoperiod plant is the potential to vegetate for an indefinite period of time (as long as the plants are kept on a light / dark cycle 18 / 6–24 / 0). This means that these plants can tolerate more errors in the growing process. It also means you can make sure your plant produces the best possible yield once flowering begins, however we'll get into that more later. All you have to do to make the phase change is set the light cycle to 12/12. This becomes even more useful as you can create unlimited clones of your optimized plant. The main drawback is that it will take around four months to achieve a substantial yield.

However, once it is done you will usually have a bigger and more powerful plant.

AUTOFLOWERING PLANTS

How they differ from photoperiod plants is written in the name. Regardless of your feeling that the plant is ready, it will start flowering at a certain time based on its genetic programming. In a way, these plants are easier for novice growers as they will have less to worry about in regards to lighting and cycle regulation. On the other hand, due to the limited vegetative phase you will have less room to make mistakes. This isn't ideal for newbies, but the fact that it only takes two months from germination to harvest is certainly palatable. Autoflowering strains tend to produce lower and less potent yields than their photoperiod counterparts, however modern advances are bridging the gap.

Chapter 7 Germination

It is often assumed that the flowering and vegetative phases are the most critical moments in the life cycle of the cannabis plant. However, even during germination the risk of failure is high, especially if the timing is not accurately calculated. By giving your cannabis seeds the best possible start, you are sure to get healthy, robust and productive plants. There are various ways to germinate small, fragile cannabis seeds. All techniques offer different probabilities of success, and have advantages and disadvantages. It is important to keep in mind that, despite having some experience in cultivation, and using first choice equipment, it is still possible that some seeds do not germinate properly. This risk of failure is perfectly natural, as seeds are living beings. At Royal Queen Seeds, we exclusively sell feminized cannabis seeds. Therefore you will not have to worry about removing the male specimens.

ELEMENTS TO CHECK ON CANNABIS SEEDS

Regardless of where you buy your seeds, we recommend that you do a light (and delicate) inspection before planting them in the ground. Generally, all seeds germinate. But poor quality seeds produce weaker plants. Unfortunately, this is a factor that you can only verify when the plant enters the vegetative and flowering phases. To avoid disappointment, remember that dark colored seeds are more likely to sprout, while light green or white colored seeds may not sprout at all. If a dark colored seed appears slightly damaged, it must be planted anyway. It is very likely that it will germinate, even if the outer shell is scratched.

TEMPERATURE PLAYS A FUNDAMENTAL ROLE IN GERMINATION

Before we look at the germination methods, here are some golden rules for proper germination. For best results, we recommend that you strictly follow these guidelines, regardless of the germination technique you choose. Of all the factors to consider, temperature is the most important element. The seeds are always looking for the slightest trace of moisture, but they use the temperature to understand when it is time to germinate.

- The ideal temperature is between 22 ° and 25 ° C
- The growing environment should be humid, but never wet
- The ideal relative humidity range is between 70% and 90%
- Seeds prefer fluorescent light (cold white code 33)
- Try to handle the seeds as little as possible
- In hydroponic / rock wool crops, the ideal pH is between 5.8 and 6.2

WHAT IS THE EXPECTED GERMINATION TIME?

The environmental factors that allow the development of the first tap root are: heat, humidity and darkness. In its constant quest for moisture, a single root will slowly develop into the gorgeous cannabis plant we all love. Under optimal conditions, seeds begin to develop within 12–36 hours after adding moisture to the environment.

Timing may vary. It all depends on the environment in which the seeds germinate (see the guidelines described above). Even the most clumsy grower can sprout a seed, but it could take a few weeks, risking getting a weak plant.

THE CHOICE OF THE GERMINATION METHOD

GLASS OF WATER TECHNIQUE

This is one of the least effective, but still valid methods. This is a very simple technique, often used by novice growers. A glass must be filled halfway with water at a temperature of about 22 ° C. After 3–5 days the seed will begin to develop, and the first white, thin roots should appear. When they reach 2–3mm in length, carefully extract the seed from the water and transfer it to a pot filled with soil. Dig small holes in the ground (about 10–15mm deep) and place the sprouted seeds inside. After placing the seeds, install a fluorescent light 13–15cm away to encourage seedling growth. Avoid giving excess water to newly developed seeds. Use a nebulizer to create a humid but not wet environment.

WET PAPER NAPKIN TECHNIQUE

This is probably the most used method. The wet napkin technique has many variations. Some growers use cotton balls or paper towels. In this guide we will use the paper towel, as it is readily available and retains moisture well. Spread a moistened kitchen paper towel on a flat surface. Deposit the seeds, spacing them a few centimeters from each other. Then, cover them with a second paper towel. Both napkins should be moist, but not wet. When the white ends of the roots reach 2–3mm, (gently) transfer the seeds to the pots. For planting, follow the procedure described above.

PLANT THE SEEDS DIRECTLY INTO THE GROUND

By planting directly in the ground, you will avoid handling and moving the seeds when they are still fragile and delicate. The first taproot is covered with microscopic filaments, easily damaged. The glass water method and the paper towel method expose the seed to temperature fluctuations. Therefore, planting directly in the ground is a much safer solution. First of all fill the pots with top quality soil, previously immersed in water. Many growers prefer to add water with a product that stimulates root growth. Make a hole 10–15mm deep. This will be the new home of your seed. Take the seed out of the package, and place it in the hole.

Cover the seed with soil, being careful not to over-compress it. The roots would penetrate the compacted soil with greater difficulty, slowing the growth of the plant. Spray the top of the soil, so that it maintains the right humidity. If you don't want to soak the soil in water, you can use a sprayer to moisten the holes before planting the seeds. With an adequate level of humidity, the roots should develop equally. The germination pots should be kept in a humid environment, at the temperature described above. After 4–10 days, the first shoots should appear, while the roots will continue to develop below the surface. At this point the plant and the soil can be transferred to a larger pot, where the actual cultivation will begin.

USE CUBES IN ROCK WOOL

Maintaining an ideal temperature (between 22 and 25 ° C), and the right level of humidity can be complicated. Leaving the seeds outdoors or on a windowsill is not the best choice; a DIY climate controlled cabinet would do a much better job. A heated mat is ideal for maintaining a constant temperature, but does not solve the moisture problem. You should therefore invest in the purchase of special equipment but by using rock wool cubes you can create a perfect environment for the germination of cannabis seeds. Immerse the cubes in water, as you would with normal soil. Rock wool retains moisture and meets the plant's water needs in the early stages of germination. After dipping the cubes, glue them to a plastic tray. Large pastry trays are perfect for this purpose.

The dome of the plastic container creates a tropical micro-climate, ideal for seeds. By placing all the components in a temperature-controlled cabinet, you will have a self-feeding source of moisture. There will be no need to handle the seeds until they become small seedlings ready to be transferred to the final growing medium. Using the rock wool cube technique, your seeds should germinate within a day or two. Two to three weeks after germination, your young seedlings should be ready for their new home. At this point you have two options: transplant them into pots with soil or face the challenge of hydroponic cultivation. You will know when your seedlings are ready to be transferred when their root system begins to protrude from the bottom of the rockwool cubes. Until they have begun to surround the bottom half of the rockwool cube, the roots will continue to search for water and nutrients in their new environment and grow downward.

Let's start

1. Gently remove the foil on the back of the package, extract the seeds and place them in a dry container.

2. You will need a shallow container, large enough to hold the germination tray. Fill the container with one liter of warm water (22-25 ° C). Pour the entire package of enzyme inside. Let the product dissolve completely, then put the tray to soak for

germination. The tray should only be submerged for 5-10 seconds. After soaking the tray, keep the liquid.

3. After removing the tray from the container, make a 10–15mm hole in each vase and carefully transfer your seeds from the dry container to the holes. Remember, one seed for each pot.

4. Using the supplied propagator, cover the bottom of the tank with a layer of perlite about 15mm high.

5. Insert the germination tray into the propagator, arrange the side walls, and place the lid. The lid has an on / off switch to turn the integrated lamp on and off.

6. Check the water levels in your tank at least once a day. The goal is to maintain a constant level. After 1–7 days, the seeds should germinate, and develop a few leaflets. When the seedling is 3mm tall, transfer it to the final growing medium.

IN DOUBT, THINK OF SPRING

Regardless of the method you decide to use, always keep in mind the environmental conditions of a spring day. In nature, cannabis seeds begin to germinate following the climatic transition from winter to spring. Humidity levels are still high, and temperatures rise. Always ask yourself the question: "Does the environment I have created for germination reflect the climatic conditions of spring?". If the answer is yes, your seeds will most likely be able to germinate.

In most cases, the seeds germinate without any difficulty. However, sometimes problems can arise. Here's how to deal with them:

LIGHTING

The first problem is light. Your seeds, or young seedlings, only need fluorescent or CFL lamps, at least at the beginning of their life cycle. Every plant needs light to survive, but excessive lighting during the first few weeks of life can be harmful.

Place the lamps 15cm away from the seeds. When the seedling begins to develop its first true leaves (with serrated edges), you can bring the lamps up to 5cm closer. If you are afraid of damaging the seedlings, insert your hand between the leaves and the lamp. If you can't stand the heat for at least ten seconds, push the light away by 2cm. Repeat this until the temperature becomes tolerable.

Young seedlings grow very quickly. Therefore, for best results, you will need to constantly adjust the distance of the lamps. After two weeks of exposure to fluorescent lights, you can switch to high pressure sodium (HPS) or metal halide (MH) lamps.

SEEDS – UP OR DOWN?

Wherever possible, the roots of a plant will always grow downward. It is not necessary to try to reposition the seed with your fingers. This is a crucial phase in the plant's life, and disturbing the seed at this stage is more harmful than beneficial. Generally, what emerges to the surface is not a root, but the stem of the cannabis plant. If you are still unsure, wait a few days and you will see the first leaves (cotyledons) appear. If all the needs of the seed have been met, the sprout will be able to grow properly. In any case, the best solution is to stay calm. Follow our "golden rules", and your young seedlings will be ready to move into larger pots in no time.

BEYOND GERMINATION

WHEN TO BEGIN ADMINISTERING THE NUTRITIONAL SUBSTANCES?

It depends on the growing medium you are using. In principle, it is not necessary to feed plants in the first 2–3 weeks of development. The soil is already rich in nutrients, and even in the coir the nutrients need to be added after about a week. If you choose to grow in hydroponics or coir, the nutrient solutions need to be boosted 0.25 times the base concentration. After the first leaves develop, increase by 0.25 for each set of leaves. For beginners, we recommend using soil as a substrate. It allows you to solve problems related to cannabis cultivation more easily. In addition, it tolerates any mistakes of the grower better. An easy way to assess a plant's nutrient needs is to look at its leaves. If food is scarce, the color of the serrated-edged leaves will turn light green. Over time, the leaves will turn yellow. This is an unmistakable sign of a nutrient deficiency. The plant won't die if its leaves turn yellow, but this symptom will remind you that it's time to feed your seedlings. Nitrogen is the substance most used by the plant during growth. When the sprout receives the necessary nutrition, its leaves will return to normal. Depending on the time elapsed before the grower intervenes, this process can take hours or days.

SIT DOWN AND RELAX

The first weeks of sprout development do not require special interventions by the grower. The nutrients, as well as the lighting, will need minor adjustments. Now that your seed has germinated, you can spend a few weeks in complete peace of mind. Sit back, relax and watch your plants grow. After these initial weeks, you can treat your seedlings as if they were in the vegetative stage by switching to an intensive lighting cycle. During germination, always remember our golden rules. If in doubt, ask yourself the question of "spring conditions". If you are sure that everything is going well, you just have to contemplate the development of your beautiful cannabis plants.

Chapter 8 The Vegetative Phase

The vegetative phase is the period of growth between seed germination and flowering. After the cannabis seeds have germinated, they will emerge from the ground in the form of seedlings. These are characterized by a very short stem and two rounded cotyledons. Then the first "real" leaves will appear. Over the course of 2–3 weeks, the seedlings will develop numerous fan leaves — necessary for photosynthesis. This event marks the beginning of the vegetative phase. The vegetative phase can last from 3 to 16 weeks (or longer), depending on the genetic makeup of the variety and the goals of the grower. During this time, explosive growth occurs. At the beginning of the vegetative phase, the plants are transferred to larger containers, to allow the root system to expand freely. The main stem grows upwards and the space between internodes increases significantly. Indica varieties keep compact size and produce numerous side branches. Sativas reach higher heights and develop fewer branches. In photoperiod plants the vegetative phase ends when the hours of light decrease.

• Outdoors, this happens when the summer passes into autumn.

• In enclosed spaces, the lighting cycle is artificially shortened to induce flowering. Plants transition from vegetative to flowering when exposed to 12 hours of light and 12 hours of darkness. Autoflowering genetics, on the other hand, flower according to their age, regardless of the lighting received.

The vegetative phase is a crucial moment in the life cycle of a cannabis plant. Growers need to create optimal environmental conditions so that the specimens grow healthy and thriving. Large sizes often equate to large yields. The larger the plant becomes, the greater the number of nodes or "tops" it will be able to develop. But size isn't the only factor. Some growers prefer to limit plant height while achieving excellent yields. This can be achieved by subjecting the specimens to special training during the vegetative phase, before the flowers begin to emerge. During the vegetative phase, the plant initiates numerous physiological processes. Fan leaves work to convert light and CO_2 into energy. The root system expands and provides a solid anchor to the plant, avoiding possible overturning; in addition, the roots absorb water and essential nutrients. To meet the particular needs of plants during this phase, growers must ensure an adequate supply of water, light and nutrients. It is also important to avoid attacks by pests and other pathogens that can damage or destroy a plantation. The vegetative phase sets the stage for the subsequent flowering. The better the state of health of the specimens during this period, the greater the chances of obtaining a lush flowering and a bountiful harvest.

HOW TO OBTAIN IDEAL VEGETATIVE GROWTH

The factors mentioned above are applicable to any cannabis plantation. If growers can achieve the perfect balance between all of these variables, they will be able to achieve vigorous growth during the vegetative phase. Even if the primary needs of plants are always the same, the differences between indoor and outdoor cultivation must be taken into account. These two environments present various obstacles to growers and their plantations.

INDOOR

In an indoor grow, plants are kept inside special tents or grow rooms — this has advantages and disadvantages. Indoor growers have almost total control over the environmental conditions during the entire life cycle of the plants. In the vegetative phase, it is possible to light the plants for 18–24 hours a day. The greater the exposure to light, the better the photosynthesis capacity of the plant will be and consequently a more explosive vegetative growth will be obtained. But this greater control implies a considerable effort. CO_2 levels, humidity and temperature must be regularly managed and measured. Growers will also need to purchase fans, hygrometers, humidifiers / dehumidifiers, vacuums and other equipment to ensure the efficiency of the grow room. It is possible to automate all of these systems through timers and sensors, but this solution is not suitable for amateur growers.

OUTDOORS

Outdoor growers have much less control over the vegetative phase and, in general, over the entire life cycle of the specimen. The plantation is at the mercy of the elements, which, in some circumstances, can be beneficial. In fact, it will not be necessary to use an artificial light source and the rains, combined with an adequate irrigation system, will eliminate the need for regular watering. To achieve luxuriant vegetative growth outdoors, it is essential to increase the natural defenses of the specimens. Many wild animals would be happy to nibble on your plants. Smaller creatures, such as insects, can gnaw leaves and chew roots, while deer and birds can damage cannabis foliage and stems. Humid environments also increase the risk of fungal infections. It is possible to adopt biological control methods, for example by introducing predatory insects to eliminate parasites, and companion plants to ward off harmful insects. Nets and fences are an effective line of defense against larger animals. Foliar sprays can help prevent mold. Growers should place the plantation in a well-ventilated area, avoiding stagnant air.

GIVE THE SEEDS AN OPTIMAL START

As mentioned above, the vegetative phase is preceded by germination. This time window is crucial for the young cannabis plant and can determine its fate. As healthy vegetative growth contributes to optimal flowering, a healthy seedling will be decisive for the entire growth cycle of the specimen. Let's take a look at the most important factors to consider during this phase.

CULTIVATION SUBSTRATE

Plants can be grown in numerous substrates, including soil and water (hydroponics). The substrate provides space for roots and — in the case of soil — also organic material and nutrients. Try adding micro-organisms such as mycorrhizal fungi to your substrate so that they create a beneficial interaction with plants. Fungi will help break down the organic material, helping to absorb nutrients. If you grow hydroponics, use good quality filtered water. Tap water can contain chlorine and other harmful substances.

LIGHTING

Light is one of the most important elements in a cannabis plantation. In addition to water and CO_2, it is an essential factor in the photosynthesis process. Growers must choose a good lighting system to allow plants to grow healthy and robust. It is advisable to use LED lights, as they save energy and reduce heat emission. During the vegetative stage, indoor photoperiod strains need 18–24 hours of light per day. The greater the exposure to light, the faster the growth will be. Many growers leave their specimens in the vegetative stage for 4–8 weeks. Thereafter, they expose them to 12 hours of light each day to stimulate flowering. Autoflowering plants, on the other hand, flower independently. It is enough to provide 18–24 hours of light per day during the vegetative and flowering stages, and observe the miracle of nature.

NUTRITION

Cannabis plants have specific nutritional needs. In the vegetative phase they need higher nitrogen doses to support the development of the stems and leaves. It also needs the right amount of potassium, to regulate the opening and closing of the stomata and produce energy. Plants in the vegetative phase also need magnesium to promote photosynthesis and calcium to keep cell walls healthy. For added convenience, growers can purchase specific nutritional formulas for the vegetative phase. There are products that provide all the necessary nutrients to plants during the vegetative phase. If you are using a hydroponic system, purchase specific nutrient solutions and administer them according to the instructions.

IRRIGATION

Water — the vital fluid. Cannabis plants need water to absorb the nutrient molecules found in soil and hydroponic plants. During the transpiration process, the water rises along the stem and reaches the leaves, carrying the nourishment where it is needed. However, an excess of water can be harmful. It can deprive the roots of air, favoring the development of root rot. When watering the plants during the vegetative phase, wait for the soil to dry completely to a depth of 3cm from the surface before giving more water. Plants grown in hydroponics will receive all the water they need directly from the substrate.

TEMPERATURE

Vegetative plants thrive at temperatures between 20 and 30 ° C. Fortunately, this is a rather large range. Plants in the vegetative stage tolerate high humidity levels. However, it is important to prevent the humidity level from falling below 40%. Temperature and humidity can be measured using a thermometer / hygrometer. Indoor growers can adjust these parameters through heaters, air conditioners, humidifiers and dehumidifiers. Outdoors, it is possible to build shelters to protect the plants in the vegetative phase from the sun, in case of violent heat waves.

VENTILATION

Ventilation is essential to keep plants in the vegetative phase healthy. Inside a grow tent, fans and aspirators will be essential for adequate air circulation, introducing CO_2 and eliminating excess oxygen. Good airflow will also prevent mold growth. If you are growing in a greenhouse, it is preferable to orient the structure towards the wind or install fans to keep the air moving.

TRAINING

The training allows growers to shape the specimens according to their needs. It allows to widen the bush, optimizing exposure to light. Training can also improve the performance of plants while at the same time containing their size. Techniques like low-stress training can be helpful in changing the shape of the plant by bending and securing the stems and branches.

THE FIRST TWO WEEKS OF THE VEGETATIVE PHASE

During this time the plants grow quickly. It is necessary to regularly check each specimen and vary the environmental parameters as needed. If you use Easy Booster Tablets, nutrient delivery will no longer be a problem. Growers also need to control the frequency of watering. It is important to wait until the first 3cm of surface soil is completely dry before adding more water. Since specimens grow very quickly, you may have to change the position of the lamps as well. If a specimen is too close to the light source, it could suffer a light burn. The lamp should be placed at a distance of 30cm from the crown of the plant. If you notice a yellowing of the leaves, you need to remove it further. During the first two weeks of the vegetative phase, it is essential to keep the humidity high. Moisture in the air can improve plant health. To do this, you can temporarily turn off the fans in your indoor grow space.

OTHER FACTORS TO CONSIDER DURING THE VEGETATIVE PHASE

In addition to the above, there are other important elements to consider during the vegetative phase, whether you are growing indoors or outdoors.

IDENTIFICATION OF THE SEX OF THE SPECIMENS

Distinguishing the sex of cannabis plants is essential to avoid the spread of male pollen in the growing area. If your goal is to get resin-rich flowers, you need to locate and remove all male specimens as soon as possible. If pollen fertilizes a female flower, it will start to develop seeds, stopping resin production. It is possible to identify the sex of the specimens about four weeks after germination. Both males and females will start producing pre-flowers — portions of tissue that indicate sex. Male plants develop spherical pre-flowers, while female pre-flowers resemble a drop. Growers can use a magnifying glass to observe the knots closely. Any male specimens should be removed from the growing area. You can keep it in a separate room for breeding projects, or dispose of it.

<u>SPACING</u>

Each specimen needs its own space. Plants that are too close together risk shadowing each other. However, many variables need to be considered. For example, the genotype of a variety affects the final size of the plant. However, it is possible to adapt the plants by applying training techniques. Growers can organize their space by calculating how many plants can be grown in each square meter. With the SOG method, 4–16 plants per m² can be planted. It is necessary to use small pots, and arrange them close to each other, so as to form a homogeneous horizontal crown. As previously mentioned, low-stress training (LST) is another widely used technique for adapting plants to your needs. It allows growers to place around four plants per m². Finally, the ScrOG method can help to increase the final yields, even if it requires only one plant per m².

PINKING

Topping is a proven technique for controlling the height of a cannabis plant while increasing its productivity. By cutting off the top of the main stem, the grower can stimulate lateral growth, maximizing yields. The topping can be applied to specimens that have developed at least 3–5 knots. This technique must be performed in the vegetative phase. Sterilized scissors should be used to remove the upper end of the stem and cause it to split. Repeat the procedure to get more buds. After each topping the plants will need some time to "recover", and this will inevitably prolong the duration of the vegetative phase.

Chapter 9 The 10 Easiest Cannabis Strains To Grow For Beginners

Grow lights, nutrients, irrigation cycles, photoperiod varieties, pest control, soil quality, hydroponic systems, drying, tanning. At first glance, the world of cannabis cultivation can seem complex, threatening and even daunting to aspiring growers. However, this activity is not necessarily difficult or complicated. First of all, ganja is a weed. If you wish, you can grow it with minimal maintenance while still managing to get a semi-decent yield. More experienced or professional growers invest large sums of money in more complex systems to harvest abundant, superior quality buds. However, if you are a beginner, you can follow various strategies to grow easily and get a good harvest. To begin, choose the most appropriate variety. By planting the right seeds, you will get the best out of the cannabis growing process. The other items you need are some good quality lamps, potting soil, fertilizer and water. Ah, and of course a little patience too!

Here is the list of the 10 easiest cannabis strains to grow.

1. Mango Sapphire

GENETICS

Indica-dominant (85%)

PARENTS Bubba's Gift

OG Afghan

THC

21-23%

CBD

0.1%

Mango Sapphire is a well known photoperiod strain that is extremely easy to grow. This indica dominant strain is descended from OG Kush, Afghani and Bubba Kush strains. The specimens develop very potent flowers, with 23% THC. The variety does not require special maintenance and is therefore suitable for beginners. First-time smokers, however, should be wary of the high generated by these buds. The effects are characterized by feelings of relaxation, calm and sleepiness. The high is accompanied by delicious, sweet and fruity aromas and flavors.

Mango Sapphire can be grown both indoors and outdoors with excellent results. Indoor specimens maintain medium size, and offer decent yields. Outdoor plants produce medium yields, but reach colossal heights of around 3m. Therefore, you need to have adequate space to keep this variety in the garden. The flowering phase lasts 7-8 weeks. Outdoor plants are ready for harvest in late September.

2. Qleaner

GENETICS

Sativa dominant (60%)

PARENTS Jack's Cleaner

Space Queen

Purple Urkle

THC

17-20%

CBD

Unknown

Qleaner is a sativa-dominant strain. It was born out of a breeding project that involved Purple Urkle, Space Queen and Jack's Cleaner genetics. This easy-to-grow plant will reward beginners with energetic and vital sativa buds that deliver a euphoric, uplifting and cerebral high. The THC content reaches 20%. This means that this strain produces fast and long-acting effects. Qleaner exudes pleasant sweet and fruity aromas. It is perfect to consume during outdoor activities such as excursions, festivals, or gatherings with friends.

This easy-to-grow photoperiod strain produces medium yields, both indoors and outdoors. Maintains small size throughout the entire growth cycle. For this reason it is ideal for those with little space available. The flowering phase of Qleaner lasts 8-10 weeks. Specimens grown outdoors can be harvested during the month of October.

3. Tropimango

GENETICS

Indica dominant (70%)

PARENTS

Somango

THC

18%

CBD

Unknown

Tropimango is one of the simplest varieties to grow ever. Lucky growers will be rewarded with buds rich in fruity and tropical aromas. The plant inherited these intoxicating flavors from the Somango strain, which is also responsible for the prevalence of indica genes in the gene pool. Tropimango develops dense and compact buds that contain THC levels of 18%. The effect is joyful and relaxing. This strain helps relieve pain and a good night's rest. Tropimango can be easily grown both indoors and outdoors. Indoor specimens offer generous yields of around 550g / m². Outdoors, up to 1800g / plant can be harvested! The flowering phase of Tropimango lasts around 8-9 weeks.

4. Easy Skunk

GENETICS

Indica dominant

PARENTS Afghani

OG Kush

Skunk 1

THC

15-18%

CBD

Unknown

The name of this variety already holds many clues. Easy Skunk inherited Skunk traits from legendary parent strains such as Skunk 1, Afghani and OG Kush. It is a delicious strain that is super easy to grow. At harvest time, buds produce an intense, indica-dominant high. Easy Skunk develops an assortment of terpenes that encompasses flavors of Cheese, Skunk and citrus. THC levels range from 15 to 18%. The high is gentle and relaxing, providing a pleasant physical sensation. Easy Skunk is another photoperiod strain that's ideal for beginners. It produces medium yields both indoors and outdoors. The indica dominance allows the specimens to maintain a compact and easily manageable stature.

5. Grandaddy Purple S1

GENETICS

Indica

PARENTS

Grand Daddy Purple

THC

Medium

CBD

Unknown

This plant is gorgeous, unique, and easy to grow. Thanks to the wonderful purple hues on the flowers and leaves, it will stand out from all other plants in the garden or grow room. Being a pure indica strain, Grandaddy Purple S1 generates an extraordinarily intense high and a strong feeling of physical high. Each hit captivates the taste buds with spicy and fruity flavors. Thanks to the medium THC levels, the effect is relaxing and calm.

Grandaddy Purple S1 specimens maintain a short stature, and can be grown easily and in complete secrecy even in confined spaces. The yields are substantial, both indoors and outdoors.

6. Allkush

GENETICS

Indica dominant (80%)

PARENTS Dutch genetics

Kush

THC

High

CBD

Low

Allkush is an award-winning cannabis strain, descended from illustrious, Kush and Dutch genetics. This indica-dominant plant relaxes the body and ignites the mind, offering calming, talkative and sociable effects. The aromas are really special, characterized by notes of musk, earth and sweetish nuances. THC levels are very high, so try not to overfill your bowls!

Indoor Allkush specimens offer substantial yields of 450g / m² and maintain a compact stature throughout the growing cycle.

Outdoors, 600g / plant can be harvested from specimens up to 2.5m tall. The flowering phase ends in 8-9 weeks.

7. Kush Cookies

GENETICS

Indica dominant (70%)

PARENTS G Kush

Girl Scout Cookies

THC

High

CBD

Unknown

Cookies Kush is a potent indica-dominant strain characterized by dark and intense shades of emerald green. The flowers are compact, slender, similar to columns. The high THC levels will satisfy even the most heavy smokers. This award-winning strain was born from the cross between OG Kush and Girl Scout Cookies strains. The high generated by Cookies Kush buds is intense, joyful and sedative, amplified by the aromas of grass, mint and earth.

Indoor yields of 650g / m² can be achieved, and equally large quantities outdoors. Specimens reach heights of 50-100cm, both indoors and outdoors, so they can be grown easily and discreetly.

8. Royal Cheese (Fast Flowering)

GENETICS

Indica dominant (60%)

PARENTS: Cheese Autoflowering

Cheese

THC

17%

CBD

Medium

Royal Cheese (Fast Flowering) is a strain suitable for the most impatient grower. It is capable of producing powerful buds in a short amount of time - after around 6 weeks of flowering. This indica-dominant plant was obtained by crossing a photoperiod Cheese and an autoflowering Cheese, accelerating the growth cycle compared to the other Cheese versions. Royal Cheese packs 17% THC and medium CBD levels. Cheese aficionados will immediately recognize its unique and pungent aroma, with surprising undertones of cheese and spice. The buds generate a calming high, which promotes a good mood.

Royal Cheese (Fast Flowering) can easily be grown both indoors and outdoors. Indoor specimens produce around 500g / m² and reach 100cm in height. Outdoors yields 600g / plant from 2m tall specimens.

9. Big Bang

GENETICS

Indica dominant (70%)

PARENTS Northern Lights

Skunk

El Niño

THC

19.8%

CBD

0.12%

Big Bang is an indica-dominant strain descended from Northern Lights, El Nino and Skunk genetics. Her buds develop almost 20% THC. The resulting high is psychedelic, relaxing and narcotic at the same time. The contrasting sweet and bitter flavors of spices and berries tickle the taste buds. Sure Big Bang brings new and stimulating sensations to the list of easy-to- grow strains. The plant maintains a low height, both indoors and outdoors. It was baptized that way because of the harvest. The buds are so abundant and full-bodied that the branches bend. The flowering phase lasts 9 weeks, and outdoor specimens are ripe at the end of September. By planting these seeds, you will get a burst of buds in the blink of an eye.

10. TNT Kush

GENETICS

Indica (90-100%)

PARENTS

Pakistani genetics

THC

18-22%

CBD

Low

TNT Kush is a 100% pure indica strain. It was bred specifically to be physically stunning with therapeutic properties. THC levels of 22% deliver an instant and persistent high. The buds give off exquisite flavors of chocolate, cherry, cypress and almond. A rich and delicious combination, appreciated by both connoisseurs and novices.

TNT Kush is a really satisfying strain for starters. It is sturdy and easy to grow, and can offer truly impressive yields. Indoor specimens can yield 550g / m², while outdoors yields around 1k / plant. This gap mainly depends on the plants being able to grow freely in height. Indoors, specimens reach 100cm, while outdoors they can reach up to 3m.

Chapter 10 How And When To Transplant Seedlings

Knowing how and when to transplant your cannabis seedlings can literally tip the scales in your favor when it comes time to harvest. Find out everything you need to know about why, when and how to transplant your cannabis.

How to transplant your cannabis: tips and advice.

Healthy roots mean strong plants and thick, resin-filled buds on your cannabis. You have to aim big — the bigger the better!

Whether you've decided to grow a SOG, a ScrOG, or are keeping things super-simple, you should transplant your cannabis into larger pots at least twice as they grow. Of course, there are some exceptions to this rule — which we'll clarify later — but first, let's ask a very important question.

WHY IS IT IMPORTANT TO TRANSPLANT CANNABIS?

Unlike hydroponic growing, growing in solid soil such as soil or coconut necessitates transplanting into larger pots as the plants grow. The reason? As the roots expand into the substrate and seek out nutrients, their web will grow to colonize as much space as possible. When the roots completely fill the volume of the pot, creating circles around the inner perimeter, growers call this "root entanglement". Vegetative growth will slow down, also limiting the potential of your crops. This can be avoided by transplanting into larger pots in advance. Transplanting ensures that the roots always have room to grow freely and vigorously.

HOW OFTEN DO YOU HAVE TO TRANSPLANT?

Plants grow faster in smaller pots, however, they are more susceptible to over-absorption of water and nutrients. When you start from small pots for seedlings or plastic cups, the risk of fungus and other growth problems is largely mitigated, but new problems arise when your future plants want to establish a strong root system. A good way to transplant is to keep seedlings in pots for planting until they have developed at least three internodes. At this point, you can transplant your specimens into larger pots, until they double in size. Finally, you will want to move your plants to the larger final containers, where they can thrive. Typically, you will need to transplant a plant (photoperiod) 2–3 times. It is not recommended to transplant frequently as it causes enough stress.

WHEN TO TRANSPLANT YOUR CANNABIS PLANTS

Let's go through a list of visual indicators that can help you determine if your plants need to be moved to larger pots!

• Plant size: If a plant has visibly outgrown the pot, it's time to transplant. Look at the number of internodes as a guideline.

• Growth rate: If you see your plant's growth accelerating in a pot that is too small, transplant it before growth becomes stunted. Keep in mind that the more leaves in your plants, the greater the photosynthesis and consequently the greater their growth.

• Root development: If the roots are tangled or come out of the pot, the plants need to be transplanted.

• Problems with watering: your growing plants will be thirsty! If the vase dries out too quickly, your ladies are likely to need a larger container.

• Growing Problems: If you observe slow growth or a diseased appearance in your plants, it could be due to the small size of their container.

HOW MUCH SPACE DOES CANNABIS NEED?

In nature, the spacing of plants affects how they grow. When cannabis is grown for industrial purposes, the plants are planted very close together. As a result, the tangle of roots releases hormones that encourage vertical growth, without many side branches. This characteristic has been exploited by humans for a long time to obtain perfect fibers, without interruptions by strong branches.

However, when growing marijuana for personal use, you generally want to give each plant more space — not just to encourage branching and robust growth, but to keep the plants healthy. So how big should your containers be at each stage of growth? As a guide to help you use your space and time efficiently, here is a list of regular pot sizes along with the growth stage in which they are typically used. In a final 30cm pot you can grow a moderate plant and in a ~ 60cm pot an exceptional plant. All regular pots are similar in that their rim diameter equals their depth. A healthy cannabis plant can easily have a canopy three times the diameter of the pot.

For seedlings and young seedlings in the vegetative phase. For robust plants in the vegetative phase. Beginning of the threshold of the final size of the pot

10cm = 0.5l   25cm = 11l   46cm = 57l

13–15cm = 1l   30cm = 19l   61cm = 95l

18-20cm = 4l   36cm = 26l   76cm = 114l

22cm = 7.5l   41cm = 38l -

WHY NOT PLANT DIRECTLY INTO THE LARGEST POT?

This is up to you to decide. However, a large pot with a lot of soil that has yet to be root colonized carries the risk of waterlogging. This means that care must be taken when watering to not create ideal conditions for mold, rot or any other type of pathogen or infection. Cannabis loves dry feet, so be careful. If you are planting directly in the largest pot, water sparingly during the first week after potting. Be aware that smaller pots are easier to care for, particularly in the first few weeks of vegetation. Small pots are also easier to move and can be easily rotated for 360 ° light coverage.

WHAT KIND OF VASES SHOULD I USE?

Most cannabis growers opt for regular white plastic pots with drainage holes in the bottom. Why the white vases? Black or other dark colors generate heat when hit by sunlight, while white containers help the soil stay relatively cool. Alternatively, some growers like to use air pots or tissue pots that naturally 'prune' roots and promote optimal health and development. For seedlings, growers tend to use plastic cups or pots designed specifically for seedlings.

The most important rule to keep in mind when transplanting is that transplant shock causes a lot of stress on plants. Pay close attention - the less damage to the roots, the better! This is not a rush operation. Another important factor is cleanliness. Make sure your work area is clean and wash your hands before handling the plants. Better still if you wear gloves.

Do not transplant during the day in the sun or an intense grow lamp. To avoid exposing your roots to excessive light, transplant at night.

TRANSPLANT: STEP-BY-STEP GUIDE

1. When transplanting seedlings, water them 1-2 days before transplanting. The soil must be moist, but not wet. For later transplants, drier soil will help the root system stay compacted.

2. Prepare the new pot by filling it with good quality soil. Do not fill it all the way and do not compact it. Water it. Make a hole in the center, large enough to fit the plant.

3. With your hand, cover the soil in the old pot (which contains your plant) and carefully turn it over. The plant should stick out between your fingers.

4. Gently pull out the clod and remove the old container. If the soil doesn't come out, gently squeeze and tap the sides of the pot to loosen the soil. If it is still stuck, place the pot horizontally on the floor and try to slide it out. If it still doesn't come out, use a knife and cut around the outside edge of the soil to clear it (use this method as a last resort). Don't grab the plant and try to force it out!

5. When the plant is finally released, hold one hand under the root ball and transfer the plant to the hole in its new container. Use additional soil to fill in the gaps. Tap the soil lightly to keep the plant in place.

6. Give the plant a light watering to help it settle into its new home. This is a good time to use a root stimulator. Root stimulators help relieve transplant shock and promote root development.

• We recommend that you prepare your new soil with Easy Boost Organic Plant Nutrition. Add about 50–100g of Easy Boost to 20l of soil. Easy Boost is an organic fertilizer that supplies your plants with nutrients for 10–12 weeks.

• How long does the transplant shock last? It depends. However, it is normal for a few days of slow or stunted growth to occur after transplantation. Allow the plants to recover for at least two weeks before inducing flowering or performing high stress training methods.

• If plants seem weak immediately after transplanting, support them with stakes.

• Sterilize old containers for reuse in the future.

DIMENSIONS OF INDOOR AND OUTDOOR VASES

When it comes to the recommended pot size, this will vary depending on whether you are growing indoors or outdoors.

Indoors, you will be limited by the size of your grow area and the number and size expected for your plants. Often, outdoor growing has fewer restrictions.

Theoretically, outdoors you could grow a plant as large as you want. This ensures that your cannabis roots can grow broadly, for the largest possible yields. On the other hand, pots that are too large are also not optimal: if the roots fail to fill a large pot, you will end up wasting nutrients.

In addition, moving large and heavy outdoor pots may become problematic. Alternatively, if you are growing in the wild you can simply plant directly into the ground. This way, the plants are not limited by the size of the pot and can reach their full potential.

What About Autoflowering Transplant?

Generally, we recommend not transplanting autos and planting germinated autoflowering seeds directly into their final pots because:

Autoflowering cannabis strains flower based on age rather than variations in their light cycle. They inherited this characteristic from Cannabis ruderalis, a particular cannabis variety native to some areas of Eastern Europe and Russia.

So while photoperiod strains flower once the days get shorter (or when you change the lighting schedule from 6/18 to 12/12), autoflowering strains flower automatically after about four weeks, although times may vary from one variety to another.

Can Young Autoflowering Seedlings Be Transplanted?

Technically yes, an autoflowering cannabis seedling can be transplanted. However, there is a drawback to doing so.

When transplanting a photoperiod strain, it typically stays in the vegetative stage for an extra week to help the plant recover from the stress of transplanting. When transplanting an autoflower, however, you don't have this luxury and the stress of transplanting will typically have a greater impact on the plant's growth and final yields.

How Does Transplanting Affect Autoflowering Cannabis Plants?

The roots of a plant are extremely sensitive. No matter the delicacy and care with which you transplant, you will always cause some stress to your plant when you move it to a new pot. On average, cannabis plants can take up to 7 days to fully overcome stress, although times can vary depending on the overall health of each plant (healthier ones will take less time to recover). Since you have no way to compensate for this stress when growing autoflowers, your plants will typically show signs of stunted growth after transplanting, which will ultimately result in less abundant and lower quality yields.

When is the Best Time to Transplant Autoflowering Cannabis Plants?

If you're transplanting an autoflower, timing is absolutely crucial to minimize the impact on your crops. Try transplanting your autoflowers once they have developed strong roots and at least 4–5 true leaves.

How to Transplant an Autoflowering Cannabis Plant

When transplanting an autoflowering cannabis plant, remember to follow these steps to minimize shock to the plant's roots.

Equipment

A clean workspace

Gardening or surgical gloves

New pots and soil

Prepare the Plants, Pots and Work Area

Avoid watering your plants on the day you transplant them, as it will be easier to remove dried soil from the pot. Also, prepare a clean work area for the transplant. A large, clean table will do just fine. Finally, prepare the new pot to place the plant. You may need to fill the bottom of the new pot with some potting soil to get the plant to the right height. Also, make sure the new pot has drainage holes.

Remove the Autoflowering from the Old Jar

To remove a plant from its pot, turn it upside down and gently squeeze the sides by massaging them or tapping the bottom and edges. Do not lift the plant by pulling it directly from the stem, you will only run the risk of damaging or breaking it!

Place the Autoflower in its New Jar

Place the plant in the new pot and fill it with potting soil up to about 2cm from the edge. Water abundantly and, if necessary, top up with more soil. Keep an eye on the plant for the next 3–7 days to see how it recovers from transplanting.

Plan Ahead to Avoid Transplantation

For best results in an autoflowering crop, we recommend planting them directly in the final pots. Most autoflowering strains grow perfectly in 11–12l pots.

While they are young, avoid watering autos with too much water so their small, delicate roots don't run the risk of drowning. Instead, mist the leaves regularly. Once they have developed some real leaves, water them if necessary.

Chapter 11 The Flowering Stage

The flowering phase has finally started. After spending weeks taking care of your plants, pruning and bending them to stimulate their vegetative growth as much as possible, it is time to intervene to help them bloom.

ENTERING THE STAGE OF FLOWERING

When plants are ready to bloom depends on a number of factors. If you are growing outdoors, your plants will only start flowering towards the end of summer, when the days are naturally shortened. If you are growing indoors, you will have much more control over the flowering phase of your plants. Most growers force their plants to bloom after about four weeks of vegetative growth, but technically you could keep them indefinitely at this stage.

As they begin to receive less light, the plants will automatically redirect their energies to the developing buds, rather than to the leaves. To get the best possible harvest, you will have to try to help them by giving them the right amount of fertilizers and light and ensuring the best environmental conditions.

FROM 1ST TO 3RD WEEK

• What to expect: Early flowering elongation, white hairs (pistils) and already perceptible aromas.

Many growers think that as soon as plants start flowering, they immediately stop growing to start producing buds. But that couldn't be further from the truth.

During the first week of flowering, or thereabouts, plants experience a period of accelerated growth with pronounced elongation. This "early flowering stretch" is completely normal as plants try to outgrow the surrounding vegetation in the fight for the sun's rays — to ensure a greater chance of reproduction. In addition, greater internodal distance means more space for future flowers and greater light penetration. The growth spurt you can expect during this first week will vary depending on the strain you are growing, but some plants can almost double in height during this time. The second week of flowering usually corresponds to the time when the plants clearly show their "sex". Long white pistils will begin to grow on female plants at the nodes (the sites from which the buds will develop). Males, on the other hand, will develop rounded pollen sacs. If you are growing regular seeds, check the sex of your plants as soon as possible and immediately separate the males from the females to avoid pollination (unless you are hybridizing, of course). By the third week, your plants will gradually stop stretching to focus all their energy on bud development. Although the inflorescences are still small, you will notice larger calyxes and the appearance of the first trichomes.

THE BEST PROCEDURES TO FOLLOW

• Fertilization: When it starts to flower, the nutritional needs of a cannabis plant changes dramatically. At this early stage, your plants will respond well to fertilizers with higher concentrations of phosphorus and potassium. Which NPK formula is best to use will be entirely up to you, but always be careful not to overdo it in this preliminary phase or you will risk burning the plants. Knowing to what extent to increase your nutrient intake will also be up to you, but we advise you to do it from the second week.

• Overfertilization / Deficiencies: Switching from vegetative to flowering fertilizers can be tricky, especially if you are a novice grower. Be sure to keep an eye on the plants for any signs of deficiency or over-fertilization (dead, burnt or yellow leaves).

• LST: Low Stress Training can be an excellent technique for shaping plants and for keeping the elongation that occurs early in the flowering phase at bay. The LST will also help you create an even canopy, ensuring that the lower buds of the plants get enough light.

• Temperature: Cannabis responds best to cooler temperatures during the flowering phase. Each plant will have different needs and each grower will have their own opinions about the best temperature to aim for during flowering. However, it is recommended to keep daytime temperatures around 26 ° C, while at night between 16 and 18 ° C. Keeping nighttime temperatures relatively low is extremely important for better bud development.

NUTRITIONAL SUBSTANCES, LIGHTING, TEMPERATURE AND HUMIDITY

NPK EC HUMIDITY TEMPERATURE (Day / Night)

About 5-10-7.

1.2-1.5

50–60% relative humidity

26 ° C / 16-18 ° C

FROM THE 3rd TO THE 4th WEEK

• What to expect: Bigger buds and more intense aromas

Between week 3 and week 4, the cannabis plants will have stopped growing altogether and will focus entirely on developing buds. You should notice how the buds start to get bigger each day, developing large calyxes, more white pistils and a light layer of trichomes. Plants will begin to release even more evident and complex aromas.

THE BEST PROCEDURES TO FOLLOW

• Fertilization: As plants develop bigger and bigger buds, they will need more nutrients. Again, the exact nutrient solution to use in this flowering phase is up to you, but make sure you pay close attention to how your plants react to any fertilizer variations. A commonly used NPK formula in the middle weeks of the flowering phase is 6-15-10.

• Humidity and air flow: It is very important to keep an eye on humidity and air flow. Stagnant and humid air creates the fertile ground for the development of mold and bacteria, as well as attracting parasites. To avoid any problems, we recommend that you keep your relative humidity at 40-50% and use fans or ventilation systems to keep the air in your grow room constantly moving.

NUTRITIONAL SUBSTANCES, LIGHTING, TEMPERATURE AND HUMIDITY

NPK EC HUMIDITY TEMPERATURE (Day / Night)

About 6-15-10

1.5 approximately

50% relative humidity

26 ° C / 16-18 ° C

FROM 4th TO 6th WEEK

• What to expect: We are now in full bloom and the buds are large and dense. The aromas are almost at their peak.

Between the 5th and 6th week, the plants will be in full bloom. Their inflorescences should by now be large, compact and full of white pistils. They will also display a thick layer of trichomes, which should release a pleasant, pungent aroma. If you haven't invested money in an extractor and an air filter yet, it might be a good time to do it.

If you take a closer look at the buds, you should notice some pretty drastic changes from what they looked like a few weeks ago. The calyxes will be much larger and the buds will have a denser, heavier appearance and texture. Some fast-flowering strains may already be close to harvest date, and if so, buds will appear even more mature (with more trichomes and darker colored pistils).

• Fertilization: This period (between 5th and 6th week) is considered to be the time of maximum flowering for most cannabis varieties. Be sure to keep an eye on all plants and watch out for any signs of nutritional deficiencies or over-fertilization. Depending on the size of the buds, you may want to fertilize once more to help the plants produce the best possible yield. Remember that plants do not require large amounts of nitrogen at this stage (more important for vegetative growth rather than flowering). In addition to phosphorus and potassium, flowering plants have higher needs for calcium.

• Stress: Whatever you do, we advise you to avoid stressing the plants during this phase. Otherwise, you will slow their growth or, even worse, trigger hermaphroditism. Stress can in fact cause flowering female plants to produce pollen, self-pollinating in a last attempt to reproduce before dying.

• Supports: You may be surprised at the weight that fresh cannabis buds can reach. If your plants struggle to support the weight of their buds, consider using bamboo rods and twine or gardening clips to keep the plants upright and prevent them from collapsing.

• Humidity and temperature: From here on, keep humidity around 30–40% to avoid problems with mold or pests. Also, keep daytime temperatures no higher than 25 ° C and night temperatures between 16 and 17 ° C.

NUTRITIONAL SUBSTANCES, LIGHTING, TEMPERATURE AND HUMIDITY

NPK EC HUMIDITY TEMPERATURE (Day / Night)

About 5-12-9

1.5-1.6

30–40% relative humidity

24-26 ° C / 16-17 ° C

FROM THE 6th TO THE 8th WEEK

• What to expect: Last weeks of flowering and harvest.

Week 6, 7 and 8 are the final stages of flowering for most varieties. At this point, the buds of the plants should be dense, compact and covered in a thick layer of trichomes. The latter should go from transparent to milky white, of which a small group could take on an amber color. This is a sign that the time has come to harvest. You can better check their maturation stage by observing them with a pocket microscope or magnifying glass. The pistils will continue to get darker even during these last few weeks, another sign that the plants are almost ready for harvest.

In recent weeks, phosphorus, potassium and calcium are still the most important nutrients. Two weeks before harvest, however, we recommend that you irrigate your plants with pH balanced water only. This will encourage them to assimilate any remaining nutrients, helping to preserve the natural flavors of the buds. During this last root wash, a few yellow leaves will begin to appear as all the remaining nutrients stored in the leaves are consumed by the plants. Again, your buds will be ready to harvest once most of the trichomes have turned milky white. Plants harvested a few days early tend to have more stimulating and euphoric effects, while those harvested a few days late tend to cause drowsiness and more relaxing sensations. Although it has not yet been confirmed, cannabis plants are believed to produce more CBN (the degraded form of THC) and myrcene towards the end of their life cycle.

• Root washing: Always remember to wash the roots with pH balanced water two weeks before harvesting.

• Humidity: Keep humidity between 30 and 40%, as a maximum. This way you will avoid problems with mold or pests.

• Bud ripening stage: Keep an eye on the plants during the two weeks following root washing. You will know that the buds are ready to be harvested using the trichome method described above.

• 48–72 hours of darkness: To increase the potency of your marijuana, try leaving your plants in full darkness for 48–72 hours before harvest. Some growers claim this trick is foolproof and can help plants produce more trichomes, resulting in more potent weed.

NUTRITIONAL SUBSTANCES, LIGHTING, TEMPERATURE AND HUMIDITY

NPK EC HUMIDITY TEMPERATURE (Day / Night)

About 4-10-7

1.7-1.8

30–40% relative humidity

24-26 ° C / 16-17 ° C

DO NOT HURRY TO COLLECT

Growers tend to get a little anxious in the final weeks of flowering. However, try to curb the enthusiasm and avoid harvesting your plants too early. While a week may seem like an insignificant amount of time, it can make a huge difference in the flavor, quality and potency of your stash. Make sure you pay close attention to your plants during their flowering cycle, be patient and you will surely be rewarded with top quality buds. If you want to know more about the last few weeks of flowering, including how to administer flowering stimulators, reduce noise, calculate the flowering phase based on pot size, and more,

Chapter 12 Harvest

The harvest may seem like the final phase of a long adventure. The buds are ripe and it's time to smoke them, right? Unfortunately, we need to be patient a little longer. There is a lot of work to be done. You will need to thin out, dry and cure the buds in order to obtain a pleasant and velvety smoke. All these actions will allow you to eliminate unpleasant flavors and keep the flowers longer.

The harvest phase is not just about removing the buds and placing them on a drying rack. Numerous factors need to be taken into account and timing is also important. Depending on when they are harvested, the buds will offer different levels of THC and tanning with the right degree of humidity will greatly affect the risk of mold developing.

This guide will help you get through each stage of the harvest correctly for powerful and delicious weed.

WHAT IS THE RIGHT TIME TO COLLECT?

In the harvest phase, you must first detach the flowers and branches from the plants. But what is the right time to do it? Well it depends. Depending on the timing, the chemical composition of your flowers will change dramatically. Anything from aroma to psychoactive effects can be adjusted based on how early or late you decide to harvest buds.

Generally speaking, each variety has specific flowering times. This data can be useful for planning the harvest, but it is not always accurate. Some environmental factors can prolong or shorten the ripening phase. Indica strains typically flower more quickly, for 6–8 weeks, while sativa strains take around 8–12 weeks.

There is also another way to know when to harvest. Some notions about the anatomy of the cannabis plant allow the grower to identify the ideal time frame. In fact, some parts of cannabis begin to change as the plant matures. Instead of relying on guesswork, you can use these botanical indicators as a benchmark. First of all, you have to learn about certain tissues, organs and glands of the plant.

THE FAN LEAVES START TO YELLOW

Yellowing leaves are usually a symptom of nutrient deficiency or the presence of parasites. However, this condition is absolutely normal at the end of flowering. The fan leaves are the largest and widest, which develop during the vegetative phase. These natural solar panels transform light into sugars, which are needed to produce energy. As harvest time approaches, these leaves will take on a yellowish tint and may even fall off. No fear.

This happens because plants direct a large part of their energy towards the flowers.

THE APPEARANCE OF TRICHOMES CHANGES

Trichomes are small mushroom-shaped glands present on the buds and surrounding leaflets ("sugary" or "resinous" leaflets). These tiny chemical powerhouses produce cannabinoids and terpenes in the form of sticky resin. In nature, such substances protect the plant from heat, predators and pathogens. For growers, however, resin is the primary focus of ganja growing.

The observation of the trichomes allows to establish when the flowers are completely ripe. By evaluating this parameter, growers will be able to harvest at the time that best suits their needs.

The trichomes are also visible to the naked eye, but it is advisable to use a special device to examine them in detail. A classic magnifying glass is perfect for this purpose and is the tool most used by those on a budget. Photography enthusiasts can take snapshots with macro lenses. This method also allows you to observe the changes in the trichomes over time. Commercial growers and those with more cash on hand can purchase a microscope. These laboratory instruments offer a very detailed view of the structure and nuances of the trichomes.

In the initial stages, the trichomes exhibit a clear and transparent color. This indicates that the glands are still young and produce low amounts of cannabinoids. The flowers are also small — a clear sign that harvest time is still far away.

Subsequently, the trichomes begin to take on a more opaque and milky appearance. This indicates an increase in cannabinoid production. Check the trichomes as the milky white color begins to predominate. Trichomes reach their maximum THC production when over half of them have become opaque. The buds harvested during this time will produce a powerful cerebral high, characterized by euphoria and vitality.

If you prefer more sedative and relaxing effects, wait until the trichomes take on an amber color. This indicates that THC levels have decreased, while the amount of cannabinol (CBN), the cannabinoid obtained from the deterioration of THC, has increased.

THE CALYXES ARE BIGGER

The calyx is the first part of the cannabis flower to emerge from the knot. This structure begins as a conglomeration of small leaves and eventually turns into the full flower. The calyx remains at the base of the top. Inside are the reproductive organs. The calyxes are the part of the flower that produces the most resin. Their role is mainly of structural support, as they prevent the buds from being torn off by the wind or by winged predators.

When the buds are close to ripening, the calyxes enlarge. They prepare to host the seeds, in case of pollination by a male specimen. Regularly examine the glasses with a magnifying glass to evaluate their size.

THE PISTILS TAKE ON A DARKER COLOR

The pistils, or stigma, are the antenna-shaped sexual organs that protrude from the calyxes. These structures have the task of capturing the pollen released by the males. They allow the fertilization of the female, which, once the mission is complete, will begin to produce seeds. Most growers try to avoid pollination of females to get top quality flowers. However, the pistils allow us to analyze the level of maturity of the plant. The youngest flowers exhibit white pistils, which gradually become darker, until they take on orange-brown shades. THC production is at its highest when 70% of the pistils have changed color. When 90% of them have turned dark, the amount of THC starts to decrease, while the CBN levels increase. However, keep in mind that these values are purely indicative.

TRY PROGRESSIVE HARVESTING WHEN THE LOWER FLOWERS ARE NOT COMPLETELY RIPE

If the flowers near the top of the plant have a significant number of dull, amber trichomes that indicate their maturity and are therefore ready for harvest, but the trichomes on the lower flowers are still perfectly transparent and far from ripe, you can use a technique called progressive harvest to make sure all of your harvested grass is perfectly ripe.

Also called a partial crop or a staggered crop, this method is so simple that you'll be surprised you haven't thought about it for yourself. Simply harvest individual shoots that are already ripe and trim the remaining branches and leaves as needed to expose the less ripe flowers to lighter and to better observe the signs that indicate when they are ready for harvest. Most indoor plants only require two progressive crop cycles about two weeks apart, but larger ones may need more time. Note that most plants mature from top to bottom because the top leaf mat gets lighter, and more lumens usually equates to faster ripening. However, each plant is an individual in itself, and you may therefore find a particular phenotype that matures from the bottom up. And some plants mature evenly from top to bottom, so they are not candidates for progressive harvest.

IT'S TRIMMING TIME

The next phase is that of trimming, or manicure. This is a necessary procedure to clean up the flowers and avoid an excess of "sugary" leaves in the jar of buds. All you need is a work surface, tray, latex gloves and scissors. There are two methods of cleaning flowers: "wet" trimming and "dry" trimming.

In wet trimming, the flowers are cleaned immediately after harvest, when the humidity in the buds is still high. This technique reduces the risk of mold, as the sugar leaves are removed before drying, preventing moisture build-up. The downside is that it is a complex procedure due to the sticky buds. Gloves are essential.

However, there is also a positive side: with the resin that adheres to the blades of the scissors you can make excellent hashish.

Dry trimming should be done when the buds have already dried. This method is recommended when the humidity in the room is low enough and the risk of mold developing is minimal. Dry trimming also allows for denser and more compact buds, an aesthetic that is highly appreciated by growers.

Regardless of the technique chosen, the procedure will be identical. You can remove the "sugared" leaves when the buds are still attached to the branches or you can remove the flowers one at a time and clean them separately. Remember to keep the "sugary" leaves aside, which can be used to make hashish or other extracts.

DRYING

The next step involves transferring the buds to the drying room. Drying cannabis is essential to remove excess moisture and prevent mold growth. Plus, smoking wet weed isn't pleasant at all. Before proceeding with drying, organize the space set aside for the operation. You can use an empty room, or the tent that previously contained the plantation. If the flowers are still attached to the branches, you will need to hang them on a laundry line. Otherwise, you can directly arrange the buds on a drying rack.

For best results, cannabis should be dried slowly. Sure, putting your buds in the oven may seem like the simplest solution, but it's a method that dramatically reduces the flavor and aroma of the weed. Terpenes, chemicals that give cannabis its distinctive fragrance, are extremely volatile and easily deteriorate when exposed to high temperatures. To start the drying process, you need to reach an ambient temperature of around 21 ° C, and a relative humidity of 50%. Use a hygrometer to measure these two parameters. If the values are too high, place fans, air conditioners and dehumidifiers. If they are too low, install a heater and humidifier.

The drying process takes 2 to 7 days. Check your flowers daily and touch them to assess the humidity level. Eventually stems and flowers, rather than flexing, will snap under the pressure of your fingers. At this point you can move on to the next step.

TANNING THE CANNABIS FOR A SMOOTHER FINISH

Have you ever tasted fabulous looking ganja only to find that the smoke was too pungent and unpleasant in your throat? This happens when cannabis is not properly cured. Tanning considerably prolongs the cultivation process, but increases the quality of the buds. This procedure removes moisture from the inside of the flowers, which cannot be achieved by drying alone.

The tanning improves the flavor of the buds and makes the smoke more pleasant and velvety. In fact, this process breaks down various molecules, such as chlorophyll, which can irritate the respiratory system.

The tanning makes the ganja more potent. Before buds are heated by smoking, vaping or cooking, THC is present in the form of THCA. This cannabinoid acid is broken down (decarboxylated) and becomes THC when exposed to high temperatures or over time. Tanning promotes this process and slowly increases THC levels.

This phase does not require special interventions. All you need is airtight glass jars to put the buds in.

Fill each jar about 75%, close with the lid and store in a cool and dark place. Initially, residual moisture will emerge from inside the buds, making them seemingly more hydrated. Open the jars for a few minutes, several times a day — this procedure is called "burping," which means letting the buds breathe — to disperse moisture outside and allow air to circulate. Repeat this for the first week.

In the second and third week, you will only have to open the jars once a day, for a few minutes. After three weeks, the flowers will be properly cured and will offer a full-bodied and velvety smoke. Some growers with a lot of patience extend the curing time to around eight weeks to maximize potency and taste. If you plan to store your weed for long periods, remember that you can extend the curing for over six months, without compromising the quality of the bud.

Chapter 13 The Lighting in Marijuana Cultivation

Below, dear reader, you will find all the information you need regarding the lighting and reflection system for growing marijuana. By following this basic guide, you will immediately understand what types of light you need to grow your cannabis at its best.

Marijuana requires a lot of light to grow healthily and to give us a high quality and abundant harvest. Outdoor growers take advantage of natural sunlight, but for indoor growers, it is not easy to take advantage of this source of natural light. It is therefore necessary to resort to artificial lights. In this chapter, we will explain the sources of artificial light to use for growing cannabis and which lamps are suitable for each stage of growth. Knowledge of this subject is essential for any hemp grower.

What are the terms to know before starting?

The most important terms when it comes to cannabis grow lighting are Lumens and Kelvins. Lumen is a unit of measurement of light that tells us the amount of visible light while the Kelvin is a unit of measurement of the temperature and therefore of the color that the lamp emits.

The light contains different bands of color and each color has a different effect on the plant favoring certain growth phases dependent on the wavelength of the light itself. Cannabis requires different wavelengths of light, therefore different types of light that we will analyze below.

Vegetative phase of cannabis

For the vegetative phase the plant requires a blue light similar to that produced by the sun at noon in summer and the recommended wavelength is 6500 K.

Flowering stage of cannabis

When your little one enters the flowering phase, she needs light similar to that found in nature in autumn which leans towards the red end of the light spectrum. At this stage we will need lamps with a spectrum of 2700K.

The brilliance

The term brilliance refers to the clarity and sharpness of the light moving away from the source, in our case the bulb. The farther you go from the source, the weaker the light becomes. The distance of the plant from the light source affects the amount of light received by it, in fact if we put it too far it will receive little light, while if we get too close to the source, we risk burning the plant thanks to the heat emitted.

Watts

The power of the light emitted will affect the amount of space that the latter can illuminate. For example, a 1000-watt light bulb illuminates a larger surface than a 600 watt one.

The amount of space to light will influence our choice on the bulb in order to guarantee us an optimal result for the growth of our marijuana plant.

HPS lamps for cannabis

HPS lamps or fluorescent tubes arc cylindrical / tubular bulbs containing inert gases inside. They are available in various ranges of wavelengths and colors, emulating the spectra emitted by the sun. Usually, HPS are used for clones or cuttings, to keep the mother plants and in the vegetative phase.

It is not advisable to use this type of lighting for the flowering stage seen that the sprouts do not receive enough light and as a result the yield will be minimal and of poor quality. The strength of the brightness of the light from fluorescent tubes degrades very quickly.

Advice for those starting with marijuana cultivation

HPS lamps distance: to make the most of the HPS lamps it is necessary to keep them 8-10 centimeters from the plant.

We recommend HPS for the vegetative phase for clones and mother plants

We do not recommend use in the flowering phase.

Average life span: 20,000 hours

HPS bulbs price: about 15 euros per tube

Pros:

Excellent for plants and clones

Low running costs

Versus:

Not good for flowering

Bad light penetration

CFL lamps for marijuana cultivation

Compact fluorescent or CFL lamps are similar to standard fluorescent tubes with the difference that they are smaller, have a different shape and boast more light output. They are available both as daylight / white light (6500 K) and as warm light (2700 K) and have the advantage of generating very little heat and therefore give the possibility to be approached to the plant without causing damage.

Advice for those starting with marijuana cultivation

If you decide to use CFL lamps for marijuana it is advisable to arrange more elements of less power, perhaps in order to cover as much space as possible for the plant, taking into account that this type of light has a low penetration.

In fact, the light source must be brought as close as possible to the cannabis plant to reduce light scattering.

CFL lamp distance: thanks to the low heat emitted by this type of lamps it is possible to have a distance of 8-10 cm between the lamp and your little one.

Average life span: 20,000 hours

CFL lamps price: from about 15 Euros (depends on the desired power)

Pros:

Good for indoor growing in confined spaces

Low initial and maintenance cost

Heats only a little

Versus:

Not suitable for large spaces

Lack of light penetration

LED lamps for cannabis cultivation

Unlike other lights with filaments, LEDs, which do not contain the filaments, have an extremely long life which makes them the best and effective choice for cultivation.

VIPAR SPECTRA 300W LED LAMP

According to many, LED cultivation is the lighting of the future for cannabis cultivation as it has very low maintenance costs, obtaining the same wavelength as fluorescent and discharge lamps with the advantage of absorbing 90% of the light produced, while in discharge lamps the plant absorbs about 10% of the light emitted.

Among the main advantages of LED lamps, we find low consumption compared to HPS lamps and in many cases the yield of grams / watt is higher. Another very important factor is the extremely reduced amount of heat which also translates into savings on the air conditioning system in summer and heating in the winter.

Compared to HPS lamps, it is possible to have the same power by approximately halving consumption, for example to have the equivalent of 600 W HPS the consumption of LED lamps will be approximately 250-300W.

LED bulbs allow you to bring the plant closer to the light source without risking burns thanks to the very low heat emission.

Average life span: 60,000 hours

Price of LED lamps: about 200-300 Euro (depends on the desired power)

Pros:

Extremely efficient

They have a fixed angle of illumination that allows the light to be concentrated in a confined space

Low heat emission and possibility to bring it closer to the plant

Versus:

They require more investment in the initial phase

HID lamps for cultivation

HID lamps or high intensity discharge lamps are the most used lamps for growing marijuana and perhaps the best as yield indoors or at home. The family of these lamps includes HMIs with metal alloys or MH and high pressure sodium or HPS.

HMI lamps produce a light spectrum suitable for both the growth phase and the flowering phase with a very good yield for cannabis plants.

MH lamps for marijuana cultivation

Metal halide or MH lamps are the most effective artificial white light source available on the market today for growing indoor marijuana for the vegetative phase. These bulbs are available in a range of sizes based on the desired wattage including: 175, 250, 400, 600, 1000, 1100 Watt. The most used by growers are the 400/600-watt lamps.

Tips for the budding grower:

The light spectrum emitted by metal halide lamps is perfect for the vegetative phase of our marijuana plant. MH bulbs have excellent brilliance but the only flaw is that they produce a lot of heat.

Average life: 10 thousand hours

Indicative price: eg. 400 watts: about 30/40 Euros

Pros:

Excellent lighting for marijuana growth and production with a perfect spectrum for plants.

Versus:

High electric bill

Low lamp life compared to other types

HPS lamps for indoor cultivation

High pressure sodium lamps or HPS is a high-pressure lamp that emits an orange spectrum of light similar to the sun's rays in autumn, i.e., about 2700 K. Like MH lamps, HPS are available in various ranges based on power although usually growers choose the 600 w one.

Tips for the budding grower:

To make the most of this type of HPS lamp, it must be used in combination with the MH bulb. In order to cover all the types of light your plant needs by keeping a 1: 1 ratio between MH and HPS lamps to grow healthy and strong and give you the yield you have always wanted.

Approximate price: HPS 400-watt lamp 30/40 Euro approx

Transformer or ballast (for discharge lamp): about 70/80 euros

Pros:

Excellent lighting for marijuana growth and production with a perfect spectrum for plants

Versus:

High electric bill

Low lamp life compared to other types

How to maximize the production of our cannabis and minimize the scattering of light

Lamp reflectors - indoor cannabis cultivation

Reflectors are very useful tools that allow you to limit the dispersion of light and direct it towards the plant so that it absorbs as much light as possible. A good reflector increases the amount of light channeled and also the brightness by limiting the dispersion of these elements.

Consequently, limiting the dispersion of lumens so precious to the plant and which contribute to a more abundant harvest.

A problem that arises when channeling the light is that heat is also channeled and therefore the grower will have to be very careful that the lamp is not too close to the plant and that there is good ventilation so that the plant is not damaged by the heat.

To increase heat loss, it is recommended to aim a fan and keep an adequate distance between the plant and the light.

Film reflectors

These reflectors are fixed to the walls to minimize light scattering and to provide more lumens to the plant and to distribute them better. This allows us to make our grow room more welcoming to our little one and to maximize the final yield.

The two types of film reflectors most used by marijuana growers are:

Reflective Mylar Film: The type most used by growers because it reflects most of the light and is easy to attach to the walls of the grow room. This support reflects 97% of the light present and makes it one of the most effective reflective materials available on the market today. Being available in different materials and formats, we must be careful to take the aluminum one and the format we see in video. We have the possibility of fixing it with adhesive tape, with pins or simply gluing it directly to the wall, paying close attention to bends and above all to breakages. Being very fragile it is subject to tearing. This material is expensive but extremely effective, it is good to always keep this support clean in order to maintain its reflectance.

White acrylic paint: it is a pigment and reflects large amounts of light limiting its dispersion and is a useful and effective choice for those on a limited budget. It reflects up to 85% of the available light. To increase its effectiveness, use on rough surfaces is recommended. Another advantage of its use is that it is easy to clean

Marijuana light cycles

Light cycles are the phases of light and dark that the marijuana plant must naturally go through in nature to reach the ripening phase in late September.

During its life the plant requires various phases of light depending on the phase in which it is located. It is essential for a cannabis grower to set up the plant according to a correct light cycle.

Missing the cycle or altering the hours of light can cause serious stress to the plant, with the risk that it will become hermaphrodite or produce few and poor-quality buds. Below you will find a table that will give you all the information you need to choose the right cycle and get the most out of your plant.

Chapter 14 How To Start Indoor Growing Tips

If you use cannabis for recreational or medical purposes, you have almost certainly considered growing for your own consumption. Fortunately, growing indoors is not as difficult as it is often described to us. Here are 10 simple steps to start an indoor cannabis crop right away:

1. FIND THE MOST SUITABLE GROWING SPACE

The first step to starting an indoor grow is to find the best place to set it up. Many first-time growers think that cannabis plants require large areas to grow in, but this is not entirely true.

In fact, you will be surprised to know that magnificent marijuana plants can be grown in almost any corner of the house, including closets, garages, basements and empty rooms.

Obviously, larger spaces offer important advantages, such as being able to give more space to plants and work with greater comfort. However, keep in mind that larger spaces also require more lighting and ventilation and, therefore, cost.

When looking for a space where you can grow indoors, remember the following points:

Cannabis plants have strict lighting requirements. In fact, they require periods of total darkness during which no light can penetrate from the outside, because it would disturb their normal development. Otherwise, the stress caused could compromise the health of the plants and their final yields.

Temperature / Humidity: Temperature and humidity are two extremely important factors to consider when growing cannabis. Always look for a space where you can easily control the temperature and humidity levels, in order to maximize the potential of the plants.

Cannabis plants require good airflow. Air circulation helps to maintain constant temperature and humidity levels inside a Grow Room. If it is missing, numerous problems could arise for the plants, such as mold and other diseases.

2. COVER THE INTERNAL WALLS WITH REFLECTIVE MATERIAL

Once you have found the most appropriate space to set up the cultivation, you will need to adapt it to satisfy the needs of the plants. The first step is to install reflective walls.

The reflective walls help direct the light towards the plants as much as possible, in order to obtain more powerful and abundant harvests of delicious buds. This essentially allows you to increase the power of the lights without increasing electricity costs.

A reflective surface can in fact increase the power of a lamp by up to 30%, as well as being extremely easy to install.

Here are some options for installing reflective walls in a grow space:

Grow Boxes: Grow Boxes are growing cabinets that are very popular with indoor growers. Internally they are already coated with reflective material and are specially designed to work with indoor lamps. This means that they will never melt due to the heat generated by the lamps and the light will always be reflected satisfying all the above requirements. Grow Boxes are also extremely easy to set up and usually come with everything you need to get great yields. Just avoid cracks or bubbles forming on the inside walls of the grow box, as they could reduce the reflectivity of your grow space.

Latex based matte white paint: Can be purchased at any paint shop and offers high levels of reflectivity (85-95%). It is also very easy to apply and does not create cracks or bubbles (as can be the case with the walls of the grow boxes where the reflectivity within the grow space can be compromised).

Panda plastic: Panda plastic is a special type of plastic that can be easily attached to the walls of a grow room, simply using nails or velcro. It also offers high levels of reflectivity similar to those of white latex matte paint (85-95%). Panda plastic, however, is quite expensive, especially if large surfaces are to be covered. Also, this plastic can melt when the temperatures of the lamps are too high. Just like for the walls of the Grow Box, also in this case we advise you to avoid bubbles or creases on the plastic.

3. AVOID LEAKS OF LIGHT

Cannabis plants are very sensitive to light, especially during periods of darkness. Any ray of light that enters the grow space during dark hours can disrupt the normal growth rate of plants and cause stress.

The possible consequences of light leaks are often discussed by cannabis growers. Some argue that even the smallest light leaks can affect plant growth, while others believe this is overestimated.

All growers should take a few minutes of their time to check for any light leaks inside their grow rooms.

Their presence can negatively affect plant growth and the quantity and quality of crops. In some cases, they can also cause hermaphroditism.

Checking for light leaks is extremely easy. If you're growing in a room, you just need to turn on the lights and step outside. If you see small glimmers of light coming out then there are leaks. On the other hand, if the light comes out of a room it means that it also enters it.

Then reverse the process. Enter the room with the lights off and check for any chinks coming from outside. Usually, you will notice gaps around doors and windows.

If you are growing in grow boxes, cabinets or any other enclosed space where it is not possible to physically enter, check for any leaks from the outside, looking for all the light rays emitted by the lamp closed inside the grow space.

If you notice any light leaks make sure you cover them. The techniques to be adopted vary according to their size and area. The most common strategies are:

Blackout film tape. It is an inexpensive and easy remedy to apply on small joints around door and window cracks, as well as on cracks and holes in reflective walls.

Panda plastic film. This material is perfect for covering larger light leaks and can be used to cover larger spaces such as entire doors and windows. It is more expensive than blackout tape but also more effective.

4. INSTALL AN AIR FILTER

Unless you are lucky enough to live in a country where cannabis cultivation has been legalized, you will most likely enjoy keeping your plantation a secret. This means minimizing plant odors.

One of the best ways to do this is to install an air filter. These devices filter the indoor growing air, eliminating all odors.

Most cannabis growers opt for activated carbon filters or air purifiers. These are the same filters normally used to filter out car exhaust odors, which means they can also effectively purify the air in your grow rooms.

The science behind these filters is pretty simple. The air passes through a filter containing activated carbon and its odors and other impurities are eliminated before escaping outside.

Normally, activated carbon filters are connected directly to the air extraction system (shown below). In this way, the hot air that accumulates inside the grow room is expelled through the filter and, therefore, purified before escaping outside.

If you are growing only 1 or 2 plants, you will probably be able to cover room odors without having to use a filter system. However, all medium to large sized grow rooms should have a high-quality filter and extraction system to avoid attracting unwanted attention.

5. INSTALL A VENTILATION SYSTEM

In the first part of this chapter, we mentioned the importance of air circulation in cannabis crops. Installing a quality ventilation system is the best way to provide your plants with fresh air throughout their growth cycle.

In nature, cannabis plants are constantly exposed to a light breeze. In this way the plants protect themselves from mold, bud rot and powdery mildew, as well as from soil flies, spider mites and more.

In addition, good air circulation also helps manage the humidity / heat rates of the growing area, reducing the humidity that could accumulate after an atmospheric disturbance such as rain. Finally, a light breeze urges the branches and stems of plants to become stronger and more robust, as a natural reaction to the force of the wind.

Although they are not affected by rain, indoor plants are susceptible to many of the pests and diseases most common in outdoor crops. So, always try to install a good ventilation system to provide your plants with the right amount of air flow.

The simplest way to increase air circulation in an indoor grow is to use fans. Most growers strategically place a number of wall fans to create a gentle, yet steady, breeze over all the tall parts of the plants.

To better manage the heat and humidity within an enclosed grow space, most growers also install an extraction system to suck in the stale, warm air that has accumulated in the room and to make room for the room. fresher air.

Many growers install air extractors above the lamp, where hot air tends to accumulate. In these cases, a few standard fans are enough to keep the air constantly moving around the room.

Here are some tips for installing fans and extractors inside a grow space:

Fans should not aim directly at plants with excessive speeds. Instead, try to create a constant flow of air around the apical parts of the plants.

Check the entire grow area after installing the fans to make sure the air reaches all corners of the room / area.

Too strong a draft can cause wind burns and stress the plants. A light and steady breeze is enough.

6. INSTALL A CULTIVATION LAMP

Lamps are the key to indoor growing. Cannabis plants require a lot of light to grow and produce large, delicious buds.

Lamps should always be installed to cover as many plants as possible. We recommend that you check the position of your plants in advance to ensure maximum light coverage.

Remember that cannabis grow lights can overheat and should be kept away from any flammable materials.

On the market you can find the most diverse lamps for cannabis cultivation. The choice mostly depends on the size of your grow room, your cannabis experience and your budget.

Here are some of the most popular lighting options among indoor growers:

Compact Fluorescent Lamps (CFLs): This is perhaps the most popular option for novice growers. They are cheap, but do not reach the same power as the professional lamps listed below.

Fluorescent lighting systems (T5 / T8): T5 and T8 fluorescent tubes are normally used for plants that require less light intensity than cannabis. Consequently, it is necessary to install them at a close distance from the apical parts of the plants to make them efficient. However, some growers get good results using these lamps.

LED grow lights: LED lights are much more expensive than their fluorescent counterparts just mentioned. However, they are also more powerful and can provide plants with much lighter when used correctly. If you decide to install an LED light, remember to check the model in order to install it correctly.

Metal halide (MH) and high-pressure sodium (HPS) lamps. They are the best lamps for growing cannabis. They are very powerful, relatively inexpensive and particularly easy to install. Most indoor growers opt for metal halide lamps or high-pressure sodium lamps.

7. INSTALL THE OTHER ACCESSORIES

So far, we have listed most of the most important equipment to install in a Grow Room. Once you've recovered these pieces, you'll need to start looking for and installing smaller accessories and equipment.

Here is a list of the extra accessories you will need to place inside your indoor grow:

Pots. The size depends on how big you want your plants to grow

Device for measuring pH. It is always recommended to measure soil pH levels to ensure the best environment for plants

Thermometer / hygrometer. To measure the temperature and humidity of the grow room

Soil / growing medium. You can find the most diverse substrates for growing cannabis. Choosing the right one depends on your growing skills and preferences

Shears. To be used for pruning plants

Sprayer. To apply pesticides

Fertilizers. To fertilize plants

Timer. To automate the control of light cycles

By following the previous 7 steps you will be able to set up a more than respectable Grow Room. Now you just have to find some plants to grow!

Start by selecting the cannabis strains you like best. There are thousands of varieties on the market, each with their own advantages and disadvantages. The choice is yours alone. It is very important to grow a strain that is good to smoke, but also suitable for your growing skills and grow room. You can easily browse the different cannabis strains using our database.

Once you have chosen the variety you need to evaluate how to get it. There are several ways to do this:

Growing from seed. This is a very common practice, but you will need to know how to properly germinate the seeds. If you choose this option, we recommend using feminized seeds to avoid male plants (unless you are considering some breeding projects).

Use cuttings. Some growers prefer to buy the cuttings directly to avoid having to germinate the seeds. If you choose this option, try to always get your cuttings from reliable sources.

9. BE PATIENT AND EFFECTIVE!

Once your seeds / cuttings have started to develop, you will have to wait patiently. Growing the best cannabis takes time and attention to satisfy all plant needs. Cannabis has 2 distinct growth stages. The vegetative phase is characterized by a vigorous growth during which the plants develop the various "sites" where the inflorescences will develop. After about 4 weeks, the plants move on to the flowering phase, during which all'energy will be devoted to the development of large and delicious buds. The finer details of cannabis cultivation may vary depending on the variety grown and the specific phenotype being worked on.

10. HARVEST

After an interval of 6 to 12 weeks, the plants are ready to be harvested.

First of all, make sure your buds have stopped producing white hairs. Your plants should have very pungent scents and their buds should be particularly large.

The white pistils will slowly begin to curl on themselves showing reddish and orange hues as the buds complete their ripening.

When 40% of the pistils have taken on darker colors, it means that the time of harvest is approaching. At this stage of ripeness, the buds harvested tend to have a more stimulating and less potent effect. Some growers prefer to wait a few more days when 50-70% of the pistils have turned dark. At this stage, the THC in the buds is at the highest level. Buds harvested after this time will have more relaxing effects. Once the inflorescences have been collected, they must be cleaned and dried. The latter process can take up to 2 weeks. Buds should always be dried slowly upside down and then stored in airtight glass jars.

Once the buds have been harvested and cured, the desired moment arrives to taste, smoke and savor the fruits of your labor!

The information given here is only intended to introduce the basics for starting a cannabis cultivation.

Chapter 15 The Most Common Beginner Mistakes

When growing cannabis, it's easy to make mistakes. Here is our Top 10 of the most common mistakes made by novice growers.

1. USE OF POOR GENETICS

Please don't do this. No matter what your growing experience is, when buying cannabis seeds with poor genetics, you will only have wasted your time unnecessarily. Poor quality genetics can be downright disappointing. As good as you are, these marijuana plants can only offer you the quality designed a priori by the genetics of the seed (and if this is not good the results will be mediocre too). Always do a thorough research before buying a seed, we will never tire of saying it.

2. USE OF A STANDARD SOIL BOUGHT IN A GARDENING CENTER

This is another mistake that is often made. Your cannabis plants need a certain balance of nutritional elements, which must be constantly balanced during the growth phases. Thinking of using standard soil to provide sufficient nutritional intake is wrong.

Learn about the nutritional needs of cannabis plants and what they really need to grow strong and healthy, using only suitable substrates for their growth. This also applies to the seed germination process and the seedling development phase. So, if you have to choose a soil for the first stages of growth, always buy a specific substrate for germination. Soil quality is key to successfully growing cannabis. One of the most common mistakes among novice growers is to overlook the importance of having a soil with the correct nutrient composition. Cannabis plants require a different ratio of nutrients at each stage of their growth cycle. In general, photoperiod varieties (plants that flower after a change in the light cycle) require higher nutrient concentrations. Even if you will have to fertilize your plants throughout their life, it will always be convenient to start with a soil rich in essential macronutrients such as nitrogen (N), phosphorus (P) and potassium (K), also known as NPK. When buying lots of potting soil, you will notice that the ratio of these three nutrients is almost always on the label.

If, on the other hand, you are growing autoflowering strains, you should know that these plants do not need that many nutrients and, therefore, require a different soil, such as a relatively low nutrient mixture consisting of 3 parts compost, 3 parts peat, 2 parts of perlite and 1 part of vermiculite. But the nutrients present within a soil are not the only important part. The soil also acts as the basis for the whole process of plant growth; it is the substance in which the roots expand, anchoring the plants to the ground. Be sure to always use soft and light soil, but fertile enough to crumble with light hand pressure. In this way you will allow the roots to grow through the soil without any obstacles, the water will evaporate at a suitable rate and the oxygen will effectively reach the root system. If the soil is too compact and clayey, the roots will not receive enough oxygen and water accumulations will lead to diseases such as root rot.

If you have a hard time finding good quality soil, some varieties are more tolerant than others.

3. LAMPS PLACED AT AN INADEQUATE DISTANCE

It is very important to place the grow lights at the right distance from the plants.

When this distance is too big, cannabis plants don't get enough light to satiate their appetite for lumens. This will cause their energy to be used primarily to reach the light, stretching the stems disproportionately.

This natural response will inevitably lead to thin, weak branching plants unable to support their own weight (not to mention the mediocre buds they will develop).

This happens when a plant has to use its energies to stretch itself in search of a distant source of light, without allocating them to a more solid structural development.

On the other hand, when the lamps are too close to the cannabis plants, there is a risk of excessively increasing the temperature. This heat could easily damage the leaves and tops of plants, even burning them completely.

4. NUTRITIONAL DEFICIENCIES AND EXCESSES IN CANNABIS

Cannabis plants are very sensitive to the amount of nutrients they bring. It is extremely easy for a novice grower to make fertilizing mistakes, which can very often lead to nutritional deficiencies or excesses.

This will only cause problems for the plantation itself. Therefore, be very careful and try to inform yourself well about the nutritional needs of a cannabis plant. These tricks will also help you understand immediately when a plant begins to lose its vigor.

5. REALIZE A CORRECT "FLUSHING" AT THE ROOTS OF THE PLANTS

Many growers are convinced that the washing of the roots, the so-called "flushing", is only an emergency maneuver to remedy any cases of over-fertilization or to rebalance the nutritional content.

While there are two good reasons for flushing, root washing is an indispensable crop step in cannabis cultivation. Many believe that this is a practice to be carried out only when the above situations appear, but this is not the case.

Proper washing of the roots, carried out in the right period of plant development, as in the last stages of ripening, can greatly improve the quality of marijuana.

In fact, the "flushing" serves to eliminate all the chemicals contained in excess in the plant. It is very important to know when to carry out a thorough wash in order to do it correctly.

6. HARVEST THE MARIJUANA TOO EARLY OR TOO LATE

A successful harvest is all about timing. If you harvest too early or too late, you run the risk of compromising all your hard work. There are a few factors that will help you determine the right time to proceed. Observe your plants closely to scrutinize every detail, perhaps with the help of a magnifying glass.

On a general level, start to keep an eye on the yellowing of fan leaves. This phenomenon occurs when nutrients are directed to the buds during flowering and will become even more pronounced once you perform the final root wash. Fear not, your plants aren't dying, they're just getting closer to harvest!

Going even more in detail, you begin to observe the pistils and trichomes. The latter are small, mushroom-shaped glands that produce terpenes and cannabinoids, such as THC and CBD. It is the trichomes that give the buds their crystalline and resinous appearance. In the first few weeks of flowering, place a magnifying glass in front of a bud and you will notice that these tiny glands have a translucent appearance. Over time, they will become progressively cloudier, until they show an amber color in their most advanced stage. If you want to get a marijuana with more stimulating effects, harvest the buds when most of the trichomes are a cloudy color. If you prefer the more relaxing and physical effects, then wait for most of the trichomes to turn amber.

You will also need to keep an eye on the pistils, which are nothing more than those long thin hairs located along the cannabis buds. These will turn from white to orange as the buds mature and you will notice that the buds will slow down as the pistils change color. Try to harvest when 70–90% of these hairs have changed color, but be sure to check the ripening stage by performing a "trichome test" as well.

7. IGNORANCE REGARDING SAFETY RULES

It might seem like a boring topic to cover, but safety in a grow room is an extremely important factor that needs to be seriously considered.

Stories of poorly set up rooms that have caused fires in homes or entire buildings are very common and are always due to the low regard for safety.

We have to think that we are dealing with heat, water and electricity, all parameters inserted in a single grow room. It is of fundamental importance not to cross these elements!

It is necessary to work in a safe area, where you can strictly isolate the cables you are using and where to keep irrigation under control, in order to guarantee profitable plant growth without ending up on all the national news (like the idiot who burned down his house because of some marijuana plant).

8. WRONG pH LEVELS

Cannabis plants require a substrate with a certain pH level in order to develop at their best. Allowing external agents to alter the correct pH values can cause numerous problems for you and your plants. This imbalance often leads to nutritional deficiencies.

So, if your plants show fertilization problems, always check the pH before making an additional nutritional supply.

Being able to keep the pH of the substrate of a Cannabis plant under control means being able to evaluate, manage and modify the different stages of its development.

9. INSUFFICIENT RESEARCH

All the problems we have discussed so far can be easily avoided by carrying out a thorough research. The cultivation of Cannabis is quite easy and simple, but you have to understand what are the elements that compose it.

First of all it is necessary to understand that even the most insignificant detail can be decisive and must never be overlooked. Many novice growers jump into this world without any knowledge, hoping that things will turn out for the best.

Remember, knowledge is power. Knowing all the steps to follow is the key to becoming an experienced cannabis grower.

10. TOO MUCH TALK

Shut up! We are aware of how irresistible the temptation to share a cultivation of healthy and strong plants with friends can be, but it is an illegal practice in many countries and it is always better to do it in absolute discretion.

One of the main causes of detention for cultivation of Cannabis is not the result of an investigation conducted by the police, suspicious of your business, but rather the too long language of people aware of your passion, which could give rise to a very dangerous chain reaction.

It's best to not tell anyone you're growing cannabis (not even your best friends).

Chapter 16 How to Make Feminized Cannabis Seeds

In nature, cannabis reproduces sexually, that is, through the pollination of a female plant with a male one, the so-called regular seeds are born from this crossing.

Regular seeds contain the chromosomal makeup of both parents, so the new specimens that will arise from the new seeds will most likely be 50% male and 50% female.

Feminized seeds guarantee 99% of female specimens, with plants that have characteristics very similar to the mother they come from, almost like a clone, guaranteeing uniform cultivation. Since the 1990s, the seeds banks that produced feminized seeds have monopolized the market due to the simplicity with which they can be grown; for example, the grower no longer has to pay attention to any male plants that could pollinate an entire crop.

CANNABIS DNA

Like humans, sex is inherited in cannabis plants. Cannabis has a chromosome set consisting of 10 pairs of chromosomes, a pair of these are called sex chromosomes because they determine the sex of a plant. In male plants this pair of chromosomes are called XY while in female ones they are called XX. Plants that are born from the cross between male and female inherit a set of 10 chromosomes, from each parent, including a sex chromosome. Female plants can only transmit one X chromosome, however, pollen from male plants can contain two types of chromosomes, X or Y. Therefore, the probability for the progeny to receive an X chromosome or a Y chromosome is 50%. The British geneticist Reginald Punnet has devised a diagram, called the Punnet square, which allows to determine the manifestation of some characters of the specimens derived from the crossing of two parents.

Feminized seeds work a little differently from what we have just explained, in fact the pair of chromosomes that determine their sex is of type XX, so how is it possible that plants born from feminized seeds do not have the XY variant typical of cannabis in nature?

THE FEMINIZED SEEDS

Two female plants are used to produce feminized seeds, one of the two plants is forced to produce male flowers, the pollen obtained from the male inflorescences is used to pollinate the second remaining female plant.

The pollen obtained from this forcing, or inversion of sex, possesses the pair of sex chromosomes of type XX, that is, a genetic heritage identical to the plant from which it was taken, therefore the progeny derived from this type of crossing will inherit chromosomes only of type X from both parents. The result is seeds that have sex chromosomes only of type XX, so the specimens that arise from these seeds are all female.

REVERSE OF SEX

There are various methods to force a female cannabis plant to produce male flowers from which to obtain pollen, this mechanism is erroneously called sex inversion, but in reality, it is a simple forcing to produce male type flowers on a plant that always keeps the same. i.e., female sex.

In nature, female cannabis plants, at the end of their life cycle, can develop male flowers to self-pollinate themselves as a survival mechanism in an attempt to give birth to new generations. This method is called "rodelization" of cannabis, it is the most natural way to obtain pollen from female plants but has drawbacks, long waiting times, low quantities of pollen produced and also not all plants have a tendency to produce male flowers.

A natural but ineffective method to reverse the sex of a plant is to subject it to certain types of stress; for example, abruptly interrupting the nocturnal phase of the flowering period with a few hours of light. Lack of water, unstable pH, absence of light or temperature are all factors that generate stress in the plant and can cause it to create male flowers.

The most effective way to reverse the sex of a plant is through the use of specific sprays. The "gibberellins" are growth hormones, the most common for the production of feminized seeds is gibberellin GA3, the plants must be pulverized with a 0.01% solution in distilled water that is 0.01 gram in 1 liter of water, for five consecutive days before inducing them to bloom. After about two weeks, the first male flowers will appear. Gibberellins are not easy to use, it is very important to apply the right dosage otherwise they are ineffective, they also cause a strong elongation of the plant.

Some seed producers use a colloidal silver solution to reverse the sex of a plant; colloidal silver is easy to find, the plants must be completely pulverized starting from two days before starting the flowering phase for about 10-20 days, until the pockets containing the pollen have formed. Plants are subjected to severe stress, losing a lot of vigor. Colloidal silver must be applied pure, with concentrations of at least 20 ppm to be effective.

Silver nitrate can also be used to induce female plants to produce male flowers. Silver nitrate is more effective when mixed with sodium thiosulfate.

The union of the two elements gives life to silver thiosulfate, known in the sector by the acronym STS, the use of a solution based on STS is the most effective and most productive way to obtain a lot of pollen from a female plant and future generations of stable seeds.

Let's examine how to create feminized seeds using STS.

PREPARATION OF THE STS

Preparing a silver thiosulfate solution at home is very simple and a few tools and materials readily available on the market are sufficient. Both silver nitrate and sodium thiosulfate can be bought on the web or at some pharmacies, both substances are quite cheap. Here is a list of the necessary material:

- silver nitrate
- sodium thiosulfate
- 2 liters of distilled water
- 2 beakers of 500 ml
- 1 1-liter beaker
- chopsticks for mixing
- latex gloves
- mask
- goggles
- dosing syringe
- precision slingbar

First you need to prepare two aqueous solutions, one based on silver nitrate and another based on sodium thiosulfate, let's see step by step:

- completely fill one of the two 500 milliliter beakers with the slingbar with distilled water , weigh 0.5 grams of silver nitrate pour the silver nitrate into the beaker containing the distilled water mix the nitrate solution with the rod for about 30 seconds of silver is ready fill the second 500 milliliter beaker completely with distilled water weigh with the precision slingbar 2.5 grams of sodium thiosulfate pour the sodium thiosulfate into the second 500 milliliter beaker mix with a clean rod for about 60 seconds the solution of sodium thiosulfate is ready for use

The two aqueous solutions just obtained must be mixed together to create silver thiosulfate:

- pour the sodium thiosulfate solution into the 1-liter beaker then pour the silver nitrate solution very slowly into the same 1-liter beaker mix the two solutions for about 1 minute

With a few small steps we have obtained our silver thiosulfate solution. Before being used, the STS must be diluted with distilled water in the ratio of 1: 9 for example 100 milliliters of STS with 900 milliliters of distilled water.

This recipe for the preparation of silver thiosulfate may be subject to variations, start trying with the doses recommended in this book and according to your needs make the necessary changes. Each cannabis strain responds differently

THE CHOICE OF PARENTS

To produce feminized seeds, at least two clones are required, both female, they can be two clones of the same variety or two different strains to create new hybrids. Using clones of the same variety is not very recommended: instability may occur in future generations; the same rule applies to humans.

Parents worthy of employment remain stable even if they are subjected to severe environmental stress. Parents who have a tendency to produce male flowers, or with hermaphroditic traits, will pass these characteristics on to future generations. Before using parents, subject them to severe environmental stress to verify their stability.

HOW TO MAKE FEMINIZED SEEDS

Once we have the two parents, we can proceed with the work. To simplify the demonstration, let's take as an example a Super Lemon Haze clone and a Cherry Marmalade clone, both female:

Prepare 1 liter of STS-based solution, in the ratio of 1: 9, pulverize the Cherry Marmalade clone completely with the STS solution, induce the Cherry Marmalade clone to bloom, at a regime of 12 hours of light and 12 hours of darkness after about two weeks the Cherry Marmalade clone begins to develop male flowers when the first male formations appear, also induce the Super Lemon Haze clone to bloom the male flowers, after about two weeks from their birth, they will begin to open releasing the desired pollen take the pollen by inserting a flowering branch in a paper bag the Super Lemon Haze between the second and the third week should have already developed enough female inflorescences, ready to be pollinated with a brush sprinkle the Cherry Marmalade pollen on the Super inflorescences Lemon Haze eliminate the Cherry Marmalade clone after about 6 weeks of pollination, the Super Lemon Haze should be evenings ready to be harvested, with the inflorescences full of ripe seeds cut the plant and dry it in a dark and dry place for at least two weeks chop the flowers with your hands into small parts and collect the seeds inside clean the seeds from the thin layer that covers them with the aid of a large mesh sieve the seeds must be dried for about two weeks in a dry place and then stored in the fridge for at least two months before making them germinate to test their work

SAFETY

Plants treated with STS should not be consumed but eliminated immediately after collecting pollen. It is important to use gloves, a mask and safety glasses when preparing and using the silver thiosulfate.

Chapter 17 Rodelization Technique

METHOD OF RODELIZATION

This is the most natural way to create feminized cannabis seeds. Basically, it consists of forcing female cannabis plants to become hermaphrodites, giving up the collection of their inflorescences. Hermaphroditism is a natural phenomenon whereby a cannabis plant specimen can become hermaphroditic when growing in particularly difficult conditions. When a plant thinks its life, cycle is coming to an end it will try to self-pollinate in a final attempt to reproduce. The same happens when the female plants are now mature. Again, once it reaches the end of its life cycle, the plant detects that it has not yet been pollinated and will therefore try to self-pollinate. This means that a mature female plant that is not harvested can become hermaphroditic, and as long as it does not come in contact with male pollen, you can rest assured that the seeds you get will be feminized.

Although rodelization is the most natural method of producing feminized seeds, it is not very reliable. In fact, giving up cutting the plants once mature does not always guarantee hermaphroditism and self-pollination.

Hermaphroditism is partly genetic and, therefore, the success of the rodelization method depends on the genetics of your plants. Some varieties will be more likely to develop seeds than others.

Chapter 18 Photosynthesis

Photosynthesis is key in cannabis cultivation. The sinsemilla simply could not survive without it. In this chapter we analyze the role of photosynthesis in the entire life cycle of cannabis: whether you grow indoors or outdoors, it is a read that you absolutely cannot miss.

Photosynthesis is the process by which algae, cyanobacteria and plants convert light into chemical energy. There are two types of photosynthesis: oxygenic and anoxygenic. The latter does not produce oxygen and is used mostly by bacteria, which is why in this chapter we will only focus on oxygenic photosynthesis. During (oxygenic) photosynthesis, plants absorb carbon dioxide and light and transform them into energy or carbohydrates necessary for growth, releasing oxygen as a by-product: real chemical-biological industries! Most plants, including cannabis, contain chlorophyll, known to most for being responsible for the typical green color of plants. Not only that: this pigmentation allows plants to use their leaves as real solar panels. Chlorophyll absorbs the blue and red radiation of light.

Photosynthetically Active Radiation, or PAR is a measure of the light a plant can actually convert. Visible light falls within the portion of the spectrum with wavelengths between 400 and 700nm. Photosynthetic Photon Flux Density (literally, "density of photosynthetic photons"), or PPFD, measured in micromoles per second ($\mu mol / s$), quantifies the number of photons that reach the plant. OK, now enough of the science: the key point is that PAR and PPFD are the most accurate measures of "photosynthetically" usable light. Most LED lighting systems are marketed under their respective PAR and PPFD.

Unlike LED systems, most grow lights, be they MH or HPS, are commercially characterized by their brightness, and lumens are a measure of this quantity. In reality, this is not a feature that can provide all the information you need, but it comes in handy when you have to choose from the many professional lamps available on the horticultural market today. Unfortunately, cannabis plants cannot photosynthesize with old incandescent lamps as effectively as they do with LEDs. This is why a 300-400W LED is compared to a 600W HPS.

The length of the light cycle is another determining factor to consider. The length of the day governs the development of the plant and determines when and how much marijuana will yield. It is not just the quality of the light that is important; Mary Jane needs to tan for a certain number of hours a day in order to unleash her full potential. Interruptions in the light cycle are particularly stressful for photoperiod cannabis plants.

VEGETATIVE GROWTH

Photoperiod cannabis strains can remain in an unlimited state of vegetative growth as long as they receive 15+ hours of light per day. Indoor growers prefer an 18-6 cycle or a continuous 24 hour cycle. Whiter lights are preferred to mimic spring sunlight, which is more unbalanced in the blue spectrum. Most growers use MH lamps, cool white CFL lamps, or full spectrum LEDs.

FLOWERING

The 12-12 lighting scheme has become the standard for indoor cannabis flowering. The decrease in the hours of light marks the transition to the flowering phase. In the outdoor case, however, the process is slower and more gradual as the days are naturally shortened after the summer solstice. At this stage cannabis mainly needs light in the red spectrum to grow buds. Yellow / orange HPS lamps are an old-school imitation of autumn light. Instead, growers using full spectrum LEDs just need to just reset the lamp timer.

WHAT ARE THE OPTIMAL CONDITIONS FOR PHOTOSYNTHESIS?

Perhaps the most comprehensive resource on photosynthesis in cannabis is the 2008 University of Mississippi study entitled "Photosynthetic Response of Cannabis sativa L. to Changes in Photosynthetic Photon Flux Density, Temperature, and CO_2 Levels", The title is almost unpronounceable, but it is a valuable read for the serious home grower.

In this study, the researchers tracked the indoor performance of 20 clones of a single Mexican mother plant, all four months old. By exposing plants to a range of temperatures, PPFDs and CO_2 concentrations, in a strictly controlled humidity environment, they identified the optimal conditions in which cannabis plants photosynthesize best. They also showed that cannabis thrives in carbon-rich environments.

In conclusion, the researchers developed the precise formula for optimal growing conditions. Home growers take note of the following excerpt from the report: "C. sativa is able to use quite high levels of PPFD and heat (high temperatures, t / n) for its gas and water exchanges, and performs even better when grown. at ~ 1500μmol m-2 s-1 of PPFD and with temperatures from 25 to 30 ° C "

CANNABIS PHOTOPERIODIC VS AUTOFLOWERING

Ruderalis is the rebellious cannabis strain that developed the autoflowering trait. In this case, there is no need for a reduction in the hours of light to trigger flowering. In fact, these varieties have a shorter life cycle of about 100 days after germination. Unfortunately, at the moment, there are no studies as reliable and serious as the one mentioned above which are able to reach exhaustive conclusions on ruderalis hybrids. However, there are rumors in the micro-grower community that prolonged exposure to light is good for autos. While these can survive even in just 8 hours of light per day, the most potent indoor autos give their best with a 20-4 light cycle from seed to harvest. Likewise, summer outdoor crops harvested in July / August usually yield the best buds in terms of both quality and quantity. It is not yet known how much blue light an autoflower really needs. Flowering starts so early that many growers use an HPS lamp for their entire life cycle. The good news is that it is only a matter of time before the scientific community begins to seriously study the photosynthesis of autoflowering cannabis.

Chapter 19 How to Produce Clones

By taking cuttings from a strong and healthy mother plant you will be able to preserve the exact genetic traits of that strain. As complex as it may seem, cannabis cloning can be easier than you think if you use the right techniques and equipment. Here's everything you need to know!

Cloning a cannabis plant might seem like a science fiction project to you, but it's actually quite simple. All you have to do is cut a portion of the branch from one of the plants and give it time to develop roots. Cannabis growers usually take their clones from mother plants (kept constantly in vegetative growth) or from young plants in the vegetative phase which will then be switched to flowering.

Cloning offers many benefits, but the main one is that it allows you to preserve the genetics of a specific plant almost indefinitely. Best of all, cloning is free!

What Are Cannabis Clones?

Cannabis clones are cuttings taken from a vegetatively growing marijuana plant. Once the roots develop, these cuttings turn into plants with the same genetics as the plant they were cut from.

If you buy cannabis seeds from a reputable and respected seedbank, each seed will contain genetics from both the mother and the father. However, once the seeds are germinated, you may find that the plants (or phenotypes) appear completely different from each other. This is because each plant can express the genetics inherited from its parents in different ways, just as you might be completely different from your sister or brother.

So, if you have a plant with particular characteristics (smells, tastes, yields, sizes, etc.) that you particularly love, cloning will allow you to preserve that genetics, crop after crop. If you still have any doubts about this process, take a look at the advantages of growing cannabis clones over seeds.

Cloning is all about capturing the best characteristics of a particular variety and, as such, you have to be quite selective in choosing which plants to get clones from.

The ideal would be to clone a plant that you particularly love. If you sprout a large number of seeds, keep an eye out for those with the best qualities: The fastest growing, the strongest, the best smelling, or the most productive. These are the parameters to use to select the best variety to clone.

Some characteristics that growers are used to looking for in mother plants include:

- Exotic or pungent aromas
- Sweet, pleasant and gritty flavors
- High potency and resin production
- Manageable heights (when growing indoors) and vigorous growth
- Fast flowering times

- Resistance to parasites, molds and other pathogens
- High yields

When starting from seeds, some growers choose to take clones from all their plants during vegetative growth. So once these first plants are harvested and dried, they only keep the healthiest clones of the plant that affected them the most.

But you can also take clones from all those vegetative plants that stand out in one of the areas mentioned above. Unfortunately, it will be difficult to determine the aromas, flavors and potency of a strain so early, which is why we recommend taking clones from all specimens in the crop and then eliminating the ones you don't want after evaluating the quality of the plants harvested.

Choose the Right Mother Plant to Clone

What Do You Need to Clone Cannabis?

A healthy "mother" plant in the vegetative phase

A clean scalpel, razor blade or sharp scissors

Substrate cubes for rooting (rock wool, etc.)

Cloning gel or powder

"Light" lighting for clones: Ideal is a low wattage CFL bulb or a special light for clones / seedlings

High-proof alcohol to disinfect instruments

How To Take A Cannabis Clone

When it comes to taking cuttings, there are a few key factors to keep in mind.

Choose the most suitable substrate for rooting

To help your clones develop healthy and strong roots, we recommend planting them in a well-ventilated substrate capable of retaining a lot of moisture. For best results, we recommend using rock wool cubes (made by melting and spinning natural rocks from which a fine thread is obtained). This material guarantees a high air flow and excellent moisture retention. Also get a plastic tray (on which to place the cubes to better retain water) and a transparent dome or a mini-greenhouse (propagator) to retain moisture around the clones.

Prepare the Tools

Cleaning is the key to harvesting and growing strong, healthy clones. So, make sure you wash your hands thoroughly and use gloves before handling the plants, as well as sterilize your razor, scalpel or scissors and the entire work area with high-strength alcohol.

When you take cuttings from a plant, both the mother and the cuttings have an increased risk of contracting bacterial infections from their surroundings. Washing your hands and sterilizing all equipment will minimize the risk of these bacteria causing problems for your cuttings (or even worse, the mother plant).

Prepare the Substrate and Rooting Gel

Once you have taken the cutting from the mother plant, you will need to act quickly. Never leave the inside of the freshly cut branch exposed to the elements for longer than absolutely necessary. To speed up the cloning process, we recommend that you set up your work area before making the cuts, with the rooting gel and substrate ready to use.

In addition, we recommend that you lightly moisten the substrate before starting cloning. Just remember not to overdo it. Clones love high humidity and a slightly moist substrate, but will rot in a water-saturated substrate.

Select the Branch to Remove

Technically, cuttings can be taken from cannabis plants in both the vegetative and flowering phases. However, cuttings taken from a flowering plant can take longer to root and tend to grow more slowly. They will also need to re-vegetate for about 2–3 weeks before they can be forced to flower again.

It is always best to take clones from the tip of a healthy branch. Remember: The healthier the branch portion, the faster it will root and grow. Generally, we recommend taking cuttings from the lower branches of plants, as they normally receive less light and produce smaller buds. Also make sure that the severed branch portions have at least two nodes.

Chapter 20 Indoor Cultivation Versus Outdoor

There are some substantial differences between indoor and outdoor cultivation. Knowing them can help you decide which type is best suited to your needs.

You are wondering whether it is better to grow cannabis indoors or outdoors, an important decision to make, as both strains show their pros and cons. The correct place to grow some cannabis plants depends a lot on the circumstances in which you are and the goal you have set for yourself. So, let's take a look at the advantages and disadvantages of these two ways of growing.

OUTDOOR

Growing cannabis outdoors is the most natural way to grow a plant (as Mother Nature would like). The only considerations to keep in mind are that growing cannabis outdoors requires places where plants can go unnoticed, 8 hours of direct sunlight, a source of water close to the plantation, and easy access to inspect at least once every 1-2 weeks.

Advantages

This is the simplest way to grow cannabis, as most of the nutrients and moisture needed by the plant are already present in the surrounding natural environment (although plants may require an additional supply of fertilizer from time to time).

Outdoors plants tend to get much larger which results in higher yields. This is due to the fact that, unlike a grow room, outdoor grown cannabis has all the space it needs to grow, under the powerful sunlight that allows it to grow strong and healthy. Just to give you an idea, direct sunlight is capable of delivering 1000 watts per square meter, often exceeding the lumen intensity of its indoor counterpart.

It is cheap! Ultimately, the only thing you need is a seed and a little water. No ventilation systems or special lamps are needed to start this type of cultivation, not to mention the total absence of costs deriving from electricity bills. With this we certainly do not mean that in outdoor cultivation there is no additional cost, indeed, many people even spend large amounts of money on planting outdoors. However, these expenses are not entirely necessary, as is the case in indoor environments.

It is quite common to think that a bud grown under sunlight gives off more heady fragrances than a bud grown indoors.

Disadvantages

Cannabis is at the mercy of several environmental factors and could be destroyed in a few hours by storms, strong winds and rain. This can be avoided by growing outdoors with normal pots, so you can put the plants in a safe place on the roughest days. However, the latter solution would limit the growth space of plants, which would lead to disadvantages in an environment which, a priori, should instead offer unlimited areas of development.

Outdoor cultivation is a difficult road for those who live in the city center or in very busy residential areas.

If the plantation is not near a water source, you will have to take care of it, carrying water as often as drought requires it.

If the cultivation area is not carefully studied, there is a risk that passers-by or, even worse, thieves may be interested in your activities.

And speaking of risks and dangers, cannabis grown outdoors is also more prone to damage from pests, animals and diseases.

Since there is no control over the hours of light provided by the sun, growing periods tend to be longer (but yields are higher).

Depending on where you live, outdoor grows tend to produce only one crop per year (unless you're using autoflowering strains).

INDOOR

Indoor cultivation is considered by many to be a much safer and more discreet practice, especially by those who live in urban areas. For indoor cannabis cultivation you need a source of electricity, water and enough space to grow at least one or two plants. The purpose of indoor cultivation is to recreate the ideal environment for a stable and controlled development of plants.

Advantages

The main advantage of growing indoors is total control of the environment in which the plants grow. Lighting, temperature, water, humidity and CO2 levels can be controlled relatively easily. Furthermore, it is also quite easy to keep pests and diseases under control.

Being able to control the lighting means managing the growth of plants to your advantage, reducing development times and starting the flowering phase at the time that best suits your needs.

A well-planned indoor grow with a good ventilation system is much more discreet than an outdoor grow.

Cannabis can be grown all year round.

Many think that cannabis grown indoors is much more potent and qualitatively superior.

Disadvantages

The initial investments to start an indoor cultivation are always greater, given the need to purchase all the necessary equipment for its correct installation.

It involves an additional expense on the electricity bill.

In indoor cultivation, much more growing care and maintenance are required than in outdoor cultivation, as moisture and nutrients are not present in the surrounding environment. However, for some, being able to control these parameters is seen as an important advantage.

The ventilation and the filtering system must always be kept perfectly functional, to ensure maximum discretion.

When it comes to growing cannabis, you have to take into consideration several factors which will largely depend on your intentions and needs. Whichever type you choose, always try to have fun and make the most of this growing experience. Growing as a hobby is an extremely rewarding practice, especially when the efforts pay off with great results!

Some argue that weed grown indoors is superior to weed outdoors, while others would not even touch weed grown indoors. What is the truth? Which herb is really better and why?

The differences between indoor weed and outdoor weed is the source of a debate that marijuana smokers, growers and so-called "connoisseurs" have likely been facing since the first seed grown indoors was born. Specifically, this age-old debate is almost never constructive. There are usually supporters or opponents of a certain type of cultivation, often with a very strong, if not biased, opinion. Some swear by what they hold most dear that one or the other type of weed is "much better" for a certain reason. However, is this really the case? Is weed grown indoors superior to weed grown outdoors or is it the other way around? Let's look at some of these arguments to find out the truth.

THE MYTH OF "GROWING FROM SEED VS. CLONES"

Some argue that the difference between weed that is grown indoors and weed that is grown outdoors is noticeable very quickly. One hypothesis is that indoor weed is normally produced by clones while outdoor plants grow more often from seed. Since the clones are an exact replica of their mothers with better genetics, the rationale given in this case is that plants grown from seed may have unwanted variations compared to their perfect indoor-grown clones. A mistake here is the assumption that all weed grown indoors comes from clones. This is by far not the case. The other misconception is that any slight variation in cannabis grown from seeds must be negative. While this can happen, it's not always a bad thing. A new phenotype that grows outdoors from a seed could also introduce positive elements to a variety. Just because there can sometimes be slight and subtle variations to the mother plant, it doesn't mean that cannabis grown from seeds is always "worse".

Weed grown indoors is grown on soil or hydroponic, while it can be assumed that cannabis outdoors is more often grown in soil. This doesn't mean much though because there are other more important things to consider, such as the type of fertilizers and other compounds used for a particular crop.

GRASS CULTIVATION HAS MANY OTHER ASPECTS BEYOND THE "INTERNAL VS EXTERNAL" FACTOR

An outdoor cultivation on land is not always and necessarily organic, while it is possible to have an organic cultivation indoors. On the other hand, this difference would also be applicable only with the belief that "organically" grown weed is "better" than, say, hydroponic-grown marijuana. However, even then, opinions tend to differ. Some prefer organically grown weed and swear it tastes better, while others say they prefer hydroponic grown weed. Again, this is about personal opinion and taste on what is "best", there is no written rule.

FERTILIZERS, PESTICIDES, FUNGICIDES, BIOLOGICAL, HYDRO ...

The differences between fertilizers obviously also apply to pesticides, fungicides and other compounds that can be used in a crop. It is true that weed outdoors are exposed to a high risk of pests, and we can assume that this type of weed will be more likely to be treated than weed grown indoors. However, even if this is assumed, this does not automatically make the weed better or worse. Some outdoor plants may have been treated with chemical pesticides, while another outdoor grower may have used organic and natural methods to keep pests away from their crops. Heck, an outdoor grower might not even care about pesticides at all.

The point here is to point out that general assumptions about a particular crop type don't get us very far in this debate. Poor soils, chemical fertilizers, or pesticides that can be responsible for sour smoke or a bad taste can be used in any weed, whether grown outdoors or indoors.

GOOD GRASS OR BAD GRASS MAY HAVE ANY ORIGIN

In conclusion, it can be said that the perceived differences in weed do not depend on whether it was grown outdoors or indoors, but rather on many other cultivation factors. In other words, good weed and bad weed can be grown by any method, since "good" or "bad" are subjective attributes anyway. It would be smart not to form an opinion based on a single experience with a bad weed, grown indoors or outdoors. Don't choose your weed based on guesswork and legends alone. Be open to trying different varieties and forming your own opinion after tasting it. You may find that whether the weed was grown indoors or outdoors isn't all that important.

Chapter 21 Growing Media

A growing medium is the material on which cannabis plants grow. There are various types, with their advantages and disadvantages, leaving the grower to choose the most suitable for their needs. Experienced growers have reached levels where they have very personal preferences for what substrate to use. Do not worry, the time will come for you too when you will be able to better understand its function and the features that best suit your needs.

The most common cultivation substrates can be divided into two main categories: substrate composed of a mixture of soil, containing all the essential elements of an organic nature (also known as soil), and substrate for hydroponic cultivation, such as clay balls or rock wool (in this case they are inert substrates, devoid of any nutritional content).

CULTURAL SUBSTRATE - SOIL

Soil is the most used growing medium in cannabis cultivation. With the term "soil" we mean the various mixes of soil easily available on the market, extremely practical to use and rather simple to maintain. However, no matter how advanced your growing skills are, if the soil composition does not meet all the needs of cannabis it will be impossible to push its potential to the limit. Only time will help you gain more experience, allowing you to better understand the true needs of a cannabis plant. One day you too will be seized by the irrepressible desire to create a mixture of soil yourself, with which to satisfy all the needs of your plants.

When using a specific soil for growing cannabis, its composition is such that it stimulates the roots of the plants to grow properly. A healthy root system needs to move around the substrate in search of water and nutrients. Furthermore, the roots must be constantly oxygenated in order to breathe. It is for this reason that, from time to time, it is advisable to allow the culture medium to dry "slightly".

When using a growing medium consisting of soil, attention must be paid to its pH levels. The pH indicates, in this case, the acidity of the soil, on a scale ranging from 1 to 14, where 1 is extremely acid, 7 is the neutral value and 14 means highly alkaline. Cannabis needs a pH close to 7 in order to develop properly.

It is also important to evaluate the proportions of the nutrients contained in the purchased soil. These values are expressed on package labels as NPK: Nitrogen (N), Phosphorus (P) and Potassium (K). These are the three main elements required by a cannabis plant, with concentrations that can fluctuate from soil to soil. Normally, a standard soil contains proportions equal to 20:20:20. In this case, it is meant that the topsoil contains 20% of each element. On the market you can find soils with different compositions.

The different types of soil to use as a growing medium

YOUR GARDEN:

Always avoid using soil from your garden, unless you are growing outdoors. Soil from a home garden certainly contains parasites, pathogens and insects, which can easily compromise the meticulously controlled environment of an indoor grow. Always buy soil from specialty stores when growing indoors.

CLAY:

Clay is an extremely hard and compact type of soil mainly composed of hydrated alumino-silicates. These tend to become particularly elastic in the presence of water, making the clay extremely easy to shape. However, cannabis has serious difficulties growing in predominantly clay soils, as their drainage is poor and their structure is too compact for a plant's roots to grow. Normally, it is mixed with other substrates to balance the final composition of the mixture.

SAND:

Sand is hardly ever used in marijuana cultivation. It is a substrate that does not retain water or the nutrients contained in it, causing them to drain so quickly that it does not give the cannabis time to absorb them. However, sand can be used effectively to balance the composition of overly compacted substrates.

SILT:

Loamy soils have properties similar to those of sand, but their appearance is more similar to that of clay. These types of substrate also lack the ability to hold water for long, but nutrients do. Silt can be added to a soil mix to balance a composition that is too compact and poorly draining. In addition, it allows the soil to better retain nutrients.

HUMUS:

Humus is an organic substance made up of decaying plant matter. It can be obtained by mixing manure and topsoil in a compost. Due to its organic nature, there is always the risk of introducing insects and pests into a Grow Room, so we strongly recommend that you only buy it in specialized stores. Most humus producers guarantee that their products are absolutely free of insects or parasites, but since they are compounds deriving from decomposition processes, there is always a margin for error.

UNIVERSAL TERRAIN:

Universal soil can be found almost everywhere. Normally, it is composed of all the substrates mentioned above, in proportions suitable for most plants, guaranteeing a good nutritional supply and an adequate structure, capable of retaining humidity and draining water. The packs of universal potting soil can change from producer to producer. The one best suited to growing cannabis contains humus, clay and sand.

MOSS:

In some stores, you can buy moss, which absorbs and retains both water and nutrients. It can be easily mixed with other growing media, but easily deteriorates after a couple of waterings, which means it needs to be replaced relatively frequently.

COMPOSITION OF THE SOIL

As we have mentioned, a soil suitable for growing cannabis should not be too soft or too compact. A balanced substrate must not hold too much water (as it happens in too compact soils), but it must not dry out too quickly (as happens in too soft soils). A soil saturated with water does not allow the roots to breathe, while one that is too draining hinders the proper hydration of the cannabis plants. Soil bags should always indicate whether it is a wet or dry substrate. Always pay attention to the instructions on the packaging and look for a good middle ground.

GROWING CANNABIS IN COCONUT FIBER

HOW COCONUT FIBER HAS CHANGED CANNABIS CULTIVATION

Coconut fiber is a growing medium made from coconut shells.

It has historically been used for its structural characteristics of solidity and stability. Coir is also a unique and effective method of growing cannabis. Coconut is a semi-hydroponic (soilless) cultivation method, and has numerous advantages associated with traditional soil cultivation.

Coir is in a sense a new cultivation method. It has only recently been used frequently. In the past, coconut fibers were simply discarded and thrown into landfills. Now, they are responsible for producing abundant cannabis plantations around the world.

COCONUT FIBER: BASIC NOTIONS

On the current market, coir is available in the form of rigid blocks made from chopped, dehydrated coconut shells and fibers, ready to use. Coconut is suitable for growing cannabis due to its humidity to ventilation ratio of 70:30.

Many novice growers who grow on soil often make the frequent mistake of overwatering the plants. Fortunately, in the case of coconut, the fibers allow adequate drainage of excess water. Hence, the problem of over-watering will be just a distant memory. Coconut retains a significant level of oxygen, which prevents the substrate from becoming too compact, and avoids the accumulation of nutrients.

HISTORY OF COCONUT

Coconut, as an effective substrate, rose to prominence in 1986 for growing roses. Growers found that coir stimulated massive root development, and the growth of perfect flowers. Despite a general ignorance of the different types of coir substrates, horticulturists immediately appreciated the potential of coir as a substrate.

Over the next few years, many growers with different backgrounds experimented with coconut fiber, with mixed results. In the late 2000s, coir was the primary substrate used in the Netherlands for growing roses and strawberries, and was equally popular in the surrounding regions as well as further afield. As cannabis cultivation expanded, resources began to dwindle. Coconut therefore became the new way to go for growing cannabis sustainably.

WHERE DOES COCONUT FIBER COME FROM?

Coconuts are native to coastal regions. They therefore contain a natural high concentration of sodium, present in the brackish air near marine areas. In the past, the first growers to discover the effectiveness of coir had to carefully rinse the substrate with pH balanced water.

If this procedure were not performed, the result would have been the destruction of the entire crop due to the toxic levels of sodium.

Nowadays, most coir producers, who focus their business on cannabis cultivation, closely supervise every aspect of production. In this way, artificial fertilizers and sodium-free products can be obtained.

Buying coir flake or block from reputable companies means buying coir that has been previously rinsed and finished with magnesium and calcium oxide, optimized for home growing.

If in doubt, you can contact the manufacturer directly and ask your questions. If you already have a bag of coir available and ready to use, you can take the prudent route and rinse it yourself.

Using water with a balanced pH, a few rinsing will suffice to remove excess salt. You can also buy a waterproof pH tester, so you can be sure of the result. Most coir falls on a pH scale of 5.2 to 6.2, which is optimal for growing cannabis.

Using coconut fiber as a growing medium offers numerous benefits. First of all, coconut is an inactive substance that promotes rapid flowering and higher yields. Unlike soil crops, coir can be watered daily. In fact, when it reaches the saturation point, it manages to eliminate excess water thanks to its natural high rate of ventilation.

Coconut fiber in its natural form contains very few nutrients. For this reason, it easily adapts to corrections made to the substrate, adjusting the results. Furthermore, coconut fiber can only absorb the nutrients dissolved in the water, leaving everything else out. The substrate perfectly retains nutrients, but will never become saturated in excess.

Compared to other cannabis growing methods, coconut fiber is very eco-friendly. With the spread of peat moss over the past decades, it has become increasingly evident that this non-renewable source was not a sustainable choice, neither environmentally nor economically.

Coir, on the other hand, is made from waste parts of the coconut, thus reducing waste and physically using fewer resources to produce the substrate.

Coir is environmentally friendly and economical for the consumer. This method allows you to grow multiple plantations using the same block of coir. Once again, the escape of excess nutrients is possible thanks to the extraordinary versatility of this substrate.

Since it is possible to get three crops from a single batch of coir, your savings will multiply over time. If you find that your coir is running low, you can rummage for pieces that are still usable, to add to traditional soil to increase ventilation.

More experienced growers who choose coconut coir know that this method promotes growth and allows for more robust root development. Growers who use coir reap the benefits of hydroponic and soil growing.

The hydroponic aspect provides coconut's spectacular ability to produce massive yields of cannabinoid-rich buds. In addition, the plants are able to grow quickly, allowing the grower to obtain various crops throughout the year.

On the soil cultivation side, the plants are kept in normal containers, which can be easily moved around the growing area to optimize light exposure, increase air circulation, etc.

Various researches have been conducted, which have shown a remarkable healthy growth rate on various plants grown on coconut fiber. In a rose study, one group was grown on coconut fiber, while another was grown on granular rockwool. The results? Roses on coconut fiber showed a marketability of flowers 16% higher than roses on rock wool, and 18% more fresh weight than their counterparts.

VARIATIONS OF COCONUT FIBER

The type of coir used for growing cannabis depends on the personal tastes of the growers. There are various substrates on the market. Flake coir is preferred as a substrate because it allows for ideal drainage and takes longer to decompose if properly cured. Flakes that have not been cured or chemically treated have a higher risk of decomposition. Therefore, they cannot be reused to their full capacity.

Another type of substrate is coconut flour, which is obtained from the separation of coconut shells into coconut fibers and coconut flour. Coconut flour is very thin and crumbles easily unless properly seasoned to make it more durable.

The pressed block of coconut is a compact and easy to use substrate. It often needs to be re-hydrated before it can be used. This process is quite simple. You need a 9–20-liter container, a sturdy bucket and water.

After rehydrating the substrate, plants can be placed there directly. Or, you can mix coconut fiber with soil, depending on the type of cultivation you intend to carry out.

PEST CONTROL

Thankfully, coir contains none of the microscopic parasites sometimes found in common potting soil. Also, pests are not attracted to coconut coir. In fact, they prefer more welcoming environments such as peat moss. The only parasite that can threaten coconut fiber is the gnat. This species prefers to lay its eggs on the surface of the coconut substrate, as it contains enough moisture to allow them to survive.

After the eggs have been laid, the larvae pose a threat to the plant growing on the infected substrate. In fact, these insects can destroy the root system and spread diseases to plants. When the gnat larvae take over the plant, eliminating them can be quite difficult. To minimize this risk, try to keep the top of the coconut substrate dry as much as possible. In this way, you will prevent the development of the larvae.

This slight lack of hydration may slow down the vegetative development of plants, but will prevent you from losing your entire crop.

BACTERIA

While coconut coir is adverse to almost all pests, it is a breeding ground for beneficial bacteria that manage to form in the roots. Keep in mind that the presence of bacteria is not always a bad thing. In fact, many types of bacteria present in the human body favor the proper functioning of the body. Coir provides an ideal environment for the development of different types of bacteria and fungi, such as bacilli and trichoderma. These micro-organisms stimulate a healthy and vigorous growth of the plant, and the development of a robust root system.

Trichoderma is particularly important because it helps fight and eliminate other types of harmful fungi, which can attack many varieties of cannabis. Despite being a parasitic fungus, trichoderma is beneficial. It forms on the roots, and protects the plant from leaf diseases. The bacilli help keep harmful insects such as caterpillars away. They act as a kind of natural defense system, together with the terpenes. Bacilli are usually extracted and used as a natural insecticide on various plant species. They also help ward off mold and botrytis. The Bacillus Pumilus species is resistant to UV rays.

COCONUT FIBER IN GROUND CULTIVATION

Coir is a perfectly effective substrate when used alone. However, it acts in excellent symbiosis with the soil, improving its ventilation and favoring an almost immediate absorption of nutrients. Coir appears to be able to hold 1000 times more air than traditional soil. In addition, it naturally contains cellulose, lignin and potassium.

Coconut fiber is low in calcium. It is often necessary to provide calcium-magnesium supplementation to increase the levels of these two minerals. A traditional coir-soil mix is made by mixing coir and perlite, in proportions set by the grower. The compound thus obtained allows to retain water, nutrients and air in optimal quantities. In addition, perlite prevents the soil from becoming excessively compact.

DISADVANTAGES OF COCONUT FIBER

In general, coconut coir as a substrate is a revolutionary growing method and is mostly associated with benefits. However, there are also some unfavorable elements associated with this substrate. In large part, the same characteristics that make coir an excellent substance are also the ones that have its drawbacks.

In fact, since coir is an inert material, growers have to manually supply all the nutrients to the plant. While this might seem like a major drawback, keep in mind that coir can handle a wide range of human errors involving plant nutrition and irrigation. Therefore, the little extra work will be worth it.

The advent of the internet has shed light on the scientific and social repercussions of coconut fiber production and its use. However, there is still a lot of definitive information on growing coconut fiber cannabis. Coir is very effective for some plants, but it doesn't always work for every species.

Regarding cannabis, there is a wide range of coconut substrates and there is a lack of general standardization. For these reasons, the results are often very varied.

LACK OF COCONUT

The popularity of coconut coir as a growing medium suddenly increased in the mid-1990s. This resulted in a shortage of raw material. Until then, producers had a substantial influx of product, thanks to the amount of discarded and unused coconut shells from other commercial activities. When the news broke, the demand for coconut varied considerably. To keep up with demand, manufacturers have begun to take shortcuts by reducing the quality, effectiveness, and safety of the product.

In practice, farmers and producers have started selling products that may have come into contact with soil, chemicals and more. They did not subject the products to the necessary checks and analyzes to ensure the highest quality and transparency of the business.

Some batches contained toxic levels of salt. In others there were herbicides and pesticides that canceled the effectiveness of the substrate.

AN IDEAL SUBSTRATE

As a cannabis grower, you absolutely need to consider the impact of your growing medium on the final crop. But it is also important to examine how it will affect the environment and the humans who will consume the final processed gems.

As negative bias towards cannabis begins to subside, more information begins to circulate on the web. By now, virtually anyone with access to cannabis seeds or clones can become a full-time home grower.

Early crop cycles can be disappointing for novice growers. However, by choosing a sustainable and effective method such as coir, you can reduce the chances of a failed crop. It will also avoid wasting hours and hours of work.

In order to get the healthiest and most robust flowers possible, take some time to do your research and purchase the type of substrate that best suits your needs.

Coir is one of the most versatile growing methods. Therefore, it allows both novice and experienced growers to learn and experiment with new effective techniques. Soil and hydroponic cultivation will likely continue to be very popular in the future as well. However, it is important to keep an eye on new and alternative techniques to push cannabis cultivation towards continuous evolution.

How to grow marijuana with the best soil? If you are faced with this choice, you are probably a novice grower, and you are still trying to figure out what is the best soil for cannabis, so that you can then proceed with the germination of your seeds and then move on to the vegetative phase. Being one of the first choices you will have to make, together with that of the seed and the pot, it is good that you know the needs of this extraordinary plant, so that you can fully satisfy them, guaranteeing you an excellent harvest.

However, you must know that the choice is not as trivial as it seems, because a lot depends on what type of plant you are growing, in what environment you are doing it, how many plants you want to grow and with which method. In fact, there are different types of substrates, some organic, others already fertilized, others still completely devoid of any nutrient substance (because they require an addition of these substances afterwards, according to the preferences of the grower). Furthermore, the soil is not the only substrate used to grow cannabis, because for example you could also opt for a hydroponic cultivation, or a cultivation with practically visible roots that live in a mainly aqueous environment, or for an aeroponic. , that is a method that foresees that the roots grow in the air without being immersed in a substrate.

If you are a newcomer to growing marijuana outdoors, or you are simply curious about how to plant marijuana, the best choice is certainly the more traditional one, namely the use of a substrate mainly composed of earth and minerals. This marijuana potting soil will allow you to allow yourself a few mistakes too many (which with hydroponics would prove fatal), it will help you with the nutrient supply your plant needs, but unfortunately it will require a little more patience to reach the fateful moment of harvest. In fact, although the soil is so simple and complete, it does not guarantee the best possible aeration, and this obviously slows down the growth times of the plants. Let's say that in this case it is good to accept the famous saying "He who goes slowly, goes healthy and goes far", because haste is not a friend of nature, just as it is not for new growers.

Although it is clear that the soil is the right substrate for us, it is not yet clear to us which is the best. The truth is that this is a far from simple question, given that there are several variables to take into account, such as the difference between feminized and autoflowering seeds, but above all the use of fertilizers in the future.

So let's see how to move and what are the best options in terms of time, safety and yield. In this chapter we will try to satisfy all your "technical" curiosities about how to grow marijuana efficiently, and how to grow a marijuana plant.

Soil for hemp and cannabis: what nutrients it should contain and how to treat it

Cannabis and hemp need certain environmental conditions to reach their maximum, and therefore we will have to start from these characteristics in order to understand what requirements the soil I want to use must satisfy.

The pH of the soil and water

What if the pH is incorrect? If the pH is low, the roots will not be able to absorb nutrients due to the bond between acid salts and fertilizers; if the pH is high, this would limit the ability of the roots to absorb water and therefore also nourishment.

Furthermore, it is also good to remember that even the water we use for irrigation can alter the pH of the soil, so we must also measure the level of acidity and basicity of the water from our tap. Finally, if we grow outdoors, even disturbances and rain showers can alter the pH of the soil, especially thanks to the direct absorption of the leaves. For this reason, it is also necessary to measure the pH level of the soil once a week, in case there has been rain.

Soil and ambient temperatures

Many people do not know that one of the most important criteria for finding out how to plant cannabis correctly and promote its growth is related to the temperature of the soil and the environment.

In particular, the temperature of the ground obviously depends on the temperature of the surrounding environment in which it is located and on the direct exposure of the sun. Its ideal temperature is between 18 and 24 degrees, but it can also withstand higher temperatures; if the temperature changes allow it. In fact, for us it is always better that I do it a little warmer than cold, since heat increases the speed of the chemical processes of the plant, while the cold would slow them down due to the lower absorption of water.

Evidently, however, it is good not to overdo it, since excesses are able to cause more prejudices than anything else! After 39 degrees, in fact, the roots of the plant begin to lose liquids too quickly, to the point where they literally start to roast. This applies to both outdoor and indoor crops, because in both cases the use of white or air-pot style pots is always recommended, since in a greenhouse the sunlight is replaced by very powerful lamps.

The nutrients needed by cannabis

Having clarified the above points, we can only get to talk about the nutrients that are necessary for cannabis and, even more directly, for the autoflowering cannabis fertilizer. But what do we mean by all this?

First of all, it is necessary to remember that in the first phase of growth, or the first two weeks or so, cannabis does not require any type of addition of fertilizers, either diluted in water or sprayed directly on the leaves. After this period, you can start transplanting the plant into new pots every time you see it grown enough, perhaps adding more fertilized cannabis soil. Always be careful not to overdo it, because an excess of nutrients could cause symptoms of plant burns.

The nutrients that ensure good growth are the following: nitrogen, potassium, phosphorus, calcium, magnesium, sulfur and iron. During the growth period it is better to prefer a greater presence in the soil of nitrogen than that of potassium and phosphorus, which instead will have to be implemented in the flowering phase, to the detriment of nitrogen, which will instead be slowly abandoned. But be careful not to overdo it with nitrogen, as this promotes growth, thus lengthening the vegetative period.

Finally, we advise you, when preparing your cannabis soil, to add horse manure as a soil improver, which has proved particularly nutritious for marijuana. As for fertilizers, if you grow indoors it is better to use liquid ones to be diluted in water, but it is not certain that you cannot produce them at home, as with soil.

Soil for cannabis: a choice based on the type of plant grown

Not all soils are suitable for all types of cannabis. In fact, a feminized cannabis strain needs a different soil than an autoflower would want. Not so much for a big difference in nutrients required, but rather for the type of cultivation we are doing. Some mixes are famous for creating the so-called "super-soils", or soils with a high content of nutrients, which are particularly suitable for fast-yielding home crops (where autoflowering is usually opted for due to its speed of growth), on the other hand, softer but more modifiable soils are preferred, for a larger and more stable cultivation of feminized plants.

How to make your own homemade cannabis soil

Some people like to discover how to grow DIY marijuana in a complete way, starting from homemade soil.

Moreover, in this regard, it should be borne in mind that preparing a homemade cannabis soil is not a particularly complex operation. Different elements are needed, perhaps not always so easily available near your home, and this is one of the reasons why it is usually the most experienced growers to produce them, as sometimes they need to use customized mixes on a specific variety.

Therefore, for new growers, we would like to recommend the purchase of a specific soil for cannabis, in one of the thousands of online stores or in your trusted grow shop. In fact, they will certainly be perfect and complete for your use, and above all they are ready for use. The only trick you can take is perhaps to add a little extra perlite to this mix, as this mineral is capable of absorbing liquids very well and thus aerating the soil and roots.

If you have decided to create your own marijuana soil, here are some tips for creating a balanced cannabis soil:

Buy a fertilizer-free, pH-neutral organic soil base (peat), which you can find in all grow shops, nurseries and / or hobby shops.

Add at least 30% coir to your blend, whether compressed or ready-to-use, to ensure optimal soil aeration.

Add organic fertilizer, natural if possible, such as cow and horse manure, vermicompost (rich in nitrogen) or bat guano (rich in phosphorus), or artificial fertilizer in powder or pellet form.

Chapter 22 Hydroponic Systems

Growing cannabis using a hydroponic technique will allow you to push your crops far beyond their natural potential. It is a system that offers numerous advantages to all growers willing to test their cultivation skills, with the possibility of obtaining exceptional yields of top-quality buds (justifying the effort and perseverance required). However, while hydroponic growing offers numerous advantages, there are also some disadvantages. This is why it is very important to understand the steps to follow before proceeding in this direction.

Hydroponic cultivation uses water as the primary growing medium. Instead of rooting in the ground, the plants are suspended in specially designed baskets filled with inert substrates (usually coir, rockwool or expanded clay balls). Here the roots grow from the bottom of the basket to a water tank below. Growers dilute all the nutrients plants need in this water during the different stages of their growth cycle.

When plants are grown in soil, they use microorganisms (including several species of fungi) to break down organic matter into usable nutrients. These molecules are then absorbed through the roots and distributed throughout the plant. In a hydroponic setup this first step is not necessary. The roots have immediate access to already broken down and assimilable nutrients. This ease of access allows plants to grow larger and faster and produce superior yields.

Growing plants without soil may seem like an innovation in recent years, but history tells us that farmers were already using hydroponic methods thousands of years ago. The technique dates back to 600 BC, when horticulturists supplied the Hanging Gardens of Babylon with water from the Euphrates River. The Aztecs also built floating hydroponic gardens on Lake Texcoco during the 10th and 11th centuries.

There are numerous types of hydroponic setups, ranging from simple Deep-Water Culture (DWC) systems to more sophisticated ebb and flow systems.

All hydroponic plants share the same basic principle: plants grow in a soil-free substrate and receive all their nutrients through a water-based solution. Different methods use different systems to provide plants with this essential nutrient solution.

DWC is the hydroponic method par excellence. It is relatively inexpensive, easy to understand, and simple to build. A DWC system consists of a tray, a tank, mesh pots, an aquarium airstone and a pump. The plants are placed in the pots and each pot is placed in the tray. The tray acts as a lid and rests on the tank. The roots will grow in the nutrient solution placed under them.

Cells in plant roots need oxygen to stay alive. In soil this is not a problem, but in water it is a little harder to breathe. The porous stone, powered by an electric pump, aerates the water and supplies the roots with a constant flow of oxygen.

Using a hydroponic system to grow cannabis is the best way to take your growing knowledge to the next level, the important thing is to make sure you know what its advantages and disadvantages are.

ADVANTAGES OF HYDROPONIC CULTIVATION OF CANNABIS

• Increase in production yields

Hydroponic cultivation allows for much higher yields in smaller spaces, increasing the ratio of grow space to final harvest. This allows the more experienced and commercial growers to obtain higher yields and, therefore, more substantial economic inputs.

• Optimal quality control

Hydroponic cultivation systems allow you to keep the quality and development of Cannabis plants under constant control. This makes it possible to obtain a higher quality of the buds produced, compared to what can be obtained by growing on the ground.

• It is a much faster system

Cannabis grown with a hydroponic system matures much faster. This means that the harvesting times will be much shorter, thus allowing you to move to a new crop more quickly. It is quite normal to talk about 6 harvests per year when adopting a hydroponic system.

• Fewer parasites, fewer diseases

Since organic substrates are not involved, most of the parasites and diseases, which find their natural habitat in the soil, do not create particular problems in this type of cultivation technique.

• Therefore, the use of pesticides is not necessary

Reducing the risk of any pest infestations means that there is no or almost no reason to use pesticides and, therefore, the quality of the final crop will be higher.

• Less stress

When a hydroponic system is properly monitored, the possibility of plants suffering from water stress is much less frequent than in soil cultivation. We are in fact considering a cultivation technique that uses only water as the main means of cultivation.

• More efficient

Cannabis plants grown using a hydroponic system make the most of the water and fertilizers provided to them, compared to growing on land. This means that not only will it be possible to achieve better results, but that there will also be no need for large amounts of nutrients.

• A much more precise method

Hydroponic systems offer much more efficient control, thus being able to adopt a fertilization program that is much more targeted to the needs of each individual variety or plant. This step obviously takes a lot of practice, but offers the most experienced growers huge benefits.

DISADVANTAGES OF HYDROPONIC CULTIVATION OF CANNABIS

• Different cultural skills and knowledge are needed

The main drawback when deciding to adopt a hydroponic system is that most of the previously reported advantages have no basis without a fair amount of knowledge and growing skills in this field. However, once you learn the strategies of hydroponic cultivation, the quality of your cannabis plants will take a step further, but to get there, a lot of patience and practice is required.

• It is not cheap

A functional hydroponic system is not cheap and the initial investment may discourage most people who grow as a hobby (especially when compared to the costs and benefits that can be obtained from growing in soil).

• Hygiene is the key

Even if the danger of diseases is minimized, they can manifest much faster in a hydroponic system. A plant disease with the root system constantly submerged in water can spread like wildfire and, once it has entered the hydroponic circuit, it will be much more difficult to eliminate. It is therefore necessary to always keep all materials as sterile and clean as possible, especially when adopting a hydroponic system in the open air.

As you may have observed, hydroponics offers many advantages, but it requires special skills, a lot of patience and a considerable capital to invest. If you are thinking of taking the plunge, make sure before doing the proper research on the subject, know all the steps to follow to grow cannabis in a hydroponic system and have a considerable capital to invest. Once you understand the tricks of this technique you will be rewarded like royalty. But first, you will need to be able to overcome these initial obstacles.

Anyone who chooses to grow with the hydroponic system must think carefully about the substrate they plan to use. These days there are tons of types available for growers. The most common types are coir, rock wool, expanded clay, various types of turf, lava stone, perlite and vermiculite. Obviously, it is important to choose the type that best fits the needs of our cultivation system. But a question arises, do we really need a substrate? What does the substrate do in practice? How does it really work?

There is a misconception among growers that the function of the substrate only has to do with the relationship between air and water of the plant's root. In reality the role of the substrate is responsible for only 15% of the growth of the plant, the other 85% is in the hands of the grower.

The substrate is a medium in which the plant grows. It is primarily a single material, sometimes a combination of materials, which manage support and aeration by retaining and distributing water for the plant. In reality, as far as the plant is concerned, the substrate must contain water, oxygen and nutrients, drain everything correctly and remain neutral, so as not to interfere with the development of the plant. For the grower, the substrate must have a number of other factors: it must be reliable, economical to use, and lightweight. It also needs to be easy to process and dispose of. Ideally it should be non-polluting and biodegradable. And if you are a perfectionist, it should also be totally natural.

DO I NEED TO USE A SUBSTRATE?

Some find all of these parameters very boring to keep in mind and respect them. So, the next question is: how necessary is the substrate anyway? Can it work without, or at least with, minimization? This is where aeroponics or aero-hydroponics starts to get interesting. This technology provides a precise answer to these questions, responding quickly: No (Or very little anyway), the substrate is hardly needed anymore! No more carrying up the stairs bag after bag of substrate, no more illegal dumps of used materials, no more substrate-related infestations, no more huge masses of stuff to clean and drag back and forth.

WHAT ARE aeroponics and aero-hydroponics?

But what are aeroponics and aero-hydroponics? Have you ever seen a growing system that sprays the feeding solution like a fine mist compared to the root feeding system? This is an aeroponic system, a technique by which water and nutrients are delivered via a high-pressure nozzle. This technique is not widely used in its pure form. While some companies like to call their systems "aeroponics," these installations are normally only seen in research institutes and universities.

Aeroponics

Aeroponics has its own advantages and disadvantages. It saturates the supply solution with oxygen, giving the roots a very healthy environment, and the most interesting application is its use in plant reproduction. But if you want to keep the plant until it is mature you will notice that the main zone develops too fast and too abundantly, at the expense of the air-based part of the plant.

This is not normally what we grow for - cannabis is not a root vegetable. However, even if you want to grow root vegetables it is not always practical, because with aeroponics, the roots tend to remain soft, as opposed to what happens when they are constantly immersed in water and never develop the crunchy quality, we are looking for in. a root, such as licorice root ...

Aero-hydroponics

Aero-hydroponics is a modification of aeroponics. It actually started in the mid-1980s, in California, where Laurence Brooke decided to try and bring hydroponics to the international market. He started with the "EGS" (Ein Gedi System), then a group developed it at the University of Davis, California, to study the oxygen level in water, which Brooke transformed into the best propagation unit up to to date: the "Rain Forest". This unit sprays water from a nozzle onto the roots, but not in the form of a mist, but more like a spinning spray.

These days there are many variations of the aero-hydroponic system on the market, some are effective, some less, depending on the experience and knowledge of the manufacturer. It is also possible to build your own aero-hydroponic system with a little help from the many magazines and books out there in hydroponic stores these days.

In aero-hydroponics the water becomes saturated with oxygen through a number of methods: spray, injection or cascade. These usually rely on a pump which compresses the water through several irrigation pipes and sprinklers, before falling back into the tank. A well-designed aero-hydroponic system must find the perfect balance between the different components and the correct proportions between the different water streams and the shapes of the various parts (pipes, tanks, sprinklers and irrigation devices).

Neither aeroponics nor hydroponics need substrate (Or very little anyway). They just need a way to support the plants, usually in the form of small coconut pots, plastic nets, or simple rubber rings. They only have water as a substrate. Now all that's left is the water and the cultivator.

One thing we know for sure is that the hardest substrate problem has been eradicated, but you are probably wondering if you can find other problems that could be just as hard ... Well, no, not really. To completely and safely exclude traditional supports, you must be absolutely sure of the water supply for the plant, have good management for the circulation of air and a neutral and clean environment. In aeroponics and aero-hydroponics this is the perfect basis: well-oxygenated water for the roots and good drainage.

When this has been said and done, the rest, again, is all in the hands of the cultivator. You have to make sure you have a well-balanced solution, complete with nutrients; a perfect EC and pH, good ventilation, an ideal temperature, a good air humidity and hygienic working methods, just as if you were to grow any other plant or with any other cultivation technique.

Some people think aero-hydroponics is a difficult technique and they are right, up to a point. The only real benefit of having a substrate is that it acts as a buffer. This means that, unlike aero-hydroponics, where the bare root parts hang unprotected, the substrate completely surrounds the roots and therefore protects them from climatic changes, such as temperature or humidity; or other "accidents" that unfortunately can happen.

This is why beginners are usually recommended to start with a substrate system and later move on to an aero-hydroponic system once they have built up some experience. Some manufacturers offer a "duo" growing system, ie with a special kit it is possible to switch from a "substrate system" to a "non-substrate" system, while gaining more confidence. They guarantee and offer their customers a fast and free technical assistance service. Even a beginner may have a choice for aero-hydroponics if he thinks it's right for him. And don't forget that whichever technique you choose, it's not just the system or the nutrient, but the grower who is responsible for the healthy development of the plant.

Chapter 23 Nutrients

Cannabis plants are nutrient sensitive, and there is a fine line between properly feeding your plants and burning them with chemicals. Find out everything you need to know about proper fertilization of cannabis plants with our guide!

Cannabis plants require three nutrients in large quantities. These are nitrogen (N), phosphorus (P) and potassium (K), they are called macronutrients and form the foundation of the health of cannabis plants. As such, these three nutrients are usually present on the fertilizer label in the form of a ratio called NPK. The higher the number for each value, the higher the concentration of that particular nutrient.

However, cannabis needs many other nutrients in order to survive and thrive. It also relies on secondary nutrients such as calcium, magnesium and sulfur to play vital roles in plant growth:

Calcium is important for cell wall development, can help reduce soil salinity and, when used as a soil improver, can improve water penetration.

Magnesium plays a key role in photosynthesis and carbohydrate metabolism and also helps stabilize plant cell walls.

Sulfur is necessary for the formation of chlorophyll, the production of proteins, amino acids, enzymes and vitamins, and to protect plants from disease.

Apart from these, plants also use many other nutrients in small amounts (micronutrients) which are however extremely important. These include boron, chlorine, copper, iron, manganese, molybdenum, and zinc. While these are not the main nutrients plants use for food, they still play very important roles in various aspects of plant health.

There are many different brands of cannabis nutrients on the market that can vary greatly.

Typically, cannabis fertilizers can vary in the following four areas:

Nutritional Value: Different brands use different nutritional ratios that they consider optimal.

Ingredients: Different brands of fertilizers can achieve the same nutrient ratios using completely different ingredients, ranging from the most chemical (or "artificial") to the most natural.

Soil or Hydroponics: Soil nutrients are very different from hydroponic (or soilless) nutrient solutions. Make sure you only use fertilizers designed for your growing medium.

Supplements: Many fertilizer brands also produce "supplements". Generally, these products contain low NPK intakes, but contain nutrients designed to promote certain aspects of growth. For example, some supplements are essentially molasses.

We recommend that you focus more on meeting your plants' demands for macronutrients and secondary nutrients before filling them with supplements. Overdoing the nutrients can cause chemical interactions or burns that can significantly affect the size and quality of the yield.

Once you've successfully fertilized your plants with these key nutrients, feel free to upgrade to a more complex fertilization program to produce bigger and more potent yields.

The nutritional needs of cannabis change depending on the stage of growth they are in.

Cannabis seedlings obtain all their nutrients from the seed and absorb water through their leaves as their root system develops (which is why it is important to keep them in a warm and humid environment).

You will not need to start feeding your seedlings until they have reached around 3–4 weeks of age, at which point they have developed 3–4 true leaves, thus entering the vegetative growth phase.

2: 1: 2 NPK Ratio

NUTRIENTS FOR CANNABIS PLANTS IN VEGETATIVE STAGE

Some growers choose to start their plants with a light fertilizer with an NPK ratio of 2: 1: 2 for a week - just as their seedlings begin to enter the vegetative growth phase. This step can be a great way to introduce your plants to their fertilizer and avoid nutrient burn. However, some growers get great results by starting their plants with a 4: 2: 3 fertilizer to kickstart the growth.

4: 2: 3 NPK Ratio

By the middle of the vegetative phase (about 6 weeks after germination), you will need to aggressively increase your plants' nutrients to help them develop strong, healthy foliage. During this stage, most growers opt for a 10: 5: 7 fertilizer.

10: 5: 7 NPK Ratio

These high nitrogen levels will help your plants produce lush green foliage and develop plenty of bud formation points in time for flowering.

Towards the end of the vegetative phase, it's a good idea to start reducing nitrogen levels and preparing plants to switch to their flowering supplement. Most growers use a 7: 7: 7 fertilizer in the last week of the vegetative stage.

7: 7: 7 NPK Ratio

Tips on fertilization during the vegetative phase:

Beginning of the vegetative phase: 2: 1: 2 - 4: 2: 3

Mid vegetative stage: 10: 5: 7

End of vegetative phase: 7: 7: 7

NUTRIENTS FOR FLOWERING CANNABIS PLANTS

Flowering cannabis plants need less nitrogen and more potassium to encourage the growth of large, resinous flowers. During the first two weeks of flowering, most growers fertilize their plants with a 5: 7: 10 fertilizer. From here on out, it's common practice to keep adjusting nutrients on all fronts, always keeping potassium concentrations higher than the rest. Mid-flowering, most growers will use a 6:10:15 nutrient solution.

5: 7: 10 NPK Ratio

During the last few weeks of flowering, growers will reduce their nutrients to smooth the transition to pre-harvest rinse. At this point, it is common to use a milder fertilizer, with an NPK ratio of 4: 7: 10.

4: 7: 10 NPK Ratio

Beginning of flowering phase: 5: 7: 10

Mid-flowering phase: 6:10:15

Mid / late flowering stage: 4: 7: 10

End of flowering phase: pH balanced rinse

Most fertilizer brands offer their customers a fertilization scheme. Understanding these charts is the key to providing your plants with the right nutrients at the right time.

Generally, a fertilizer table has a growth cycle of 12–13 weeks. The weeks in the cycle are usually listed along the x-axis of the graph, which may also include information such as the photoperiod for each week and more.

Most importantly, your fertilization scheme will indicate which nutrients you will need to provide your plants (and in what ratio) during the different weeks of their life cycle. Nutrients are generally applied once a week and most brands of fertilizer provide a ratio of fertilizer to water (in liters or gallons). Some fertilization schemes may also provide a PPM range for their solutions. If so, invest in a PPM tester and measure the nutrients before fertilizing for greater accuracy.

Once you have fertilized your plants, it is always a good idea to check the PPM and conductivity of your soil to make sure the plants are absorbing nutrients properly.

HOW TO PREPARE THE NUTRIENTS OF CANNABIS

A potential misstep in fertilization can completely hinder your crop. However, feeding your cannabis plants can be very simple. Just follow these simple steps:

Prepare your water. If possible, heat the water to around 22 ° C to increase root absorption.

Add your nutrients according to the fertilizer instructions and mix. Use a PPM or EC meter to get correct readings.

If necessary, adjust the pH of your solution using a pH regulator in the form of nitric or phosphoric acid.

Once the PPM, pH and water temperature are correct, fertilize the plants and measure runoff using the PPM or EC meter to make sure the plants are properly absorbing their nutrients.

THE IMPORTANCE OF PPM, PH AND WATER TEMPERATURE

PPM, or parts per million, is a measure of how many nutrients are present in the water or growing medium. To avoid over or under fertilizer for your plants, it is a good idea to always measure the PPM of the soil (or growing medium) to check if it still contains any nutrients. If nutrients are present in the substrate at the time of fertilization, subtract the PPM of the substrate from the PPM recommended in your fertilization chart to avoid over fertilizer.

PH and temperature are equally important parameters when it comes to fertilizing plants. If one is even slightly out of place, your plants may have a hard time absorbing their nutrients. So whenever it's time to fertilize, keep your nutrient solution at the pH suggested by your fertilizer brand and the water temperature at 22 ° C.

TIPS FOR BETTER FERTILIZATION

Here are some quick tips to make sure your fertilization runs smoothly.

Adopt chelation

Most of the high-quality nutrients will contain chemical chelates. If you are an organic grower, you can use natural chelates such as fulvic and humic acids to help your plants absorb mineral nutrients like iron or zinc better. Chelates work by surrounding positively charged nutrients with a negative or neutral charge, allowing them to pass through the plant's pore barrier.

Try foliar fertilization

Foliar fertilization - aka spraying cannabis leaves - can be a great way to address nutritional deficiencies or pests / diseases. It is also particularly effective as a short-term fertilization with secondary nutrients such as magnesium and calcium, or micronutrients such as zinc, iron and manganese.

Always rinse

Nutrients are extremely important, but it's best to avoid them remaining in the buds when harvested. This is why it is important to rinse plants with neutral pH water at least a week before harvest. Rinsing forces your plants to consume any remaining nutrients they have stored, resulting in a soft, clean smoke.

RECOGNIZE THE NUTRIENT RELATED PROBLEMS OF CANNABIS

Excess or deficiency of nutrients can stress and damage cannabis plants. Be sure to keep your eyes peeled for the following nutrient-related issues.

pH IMBALANCE

pH problems can be caused by imbalances in your substrate, water and nutrients.

pH imbalances can have a dramatic impact on plant health and cause many other problems, such as nutrient blockage, deficiencies and more.

If left untreated, pH problems will greatly hinder plant growth and reduce both the size and quality of the crop.

NUTRIENT BURNING

Nutrient burn is usually caused by an excess or accumulation of nutrients in the growing medium.

Plants develop dark green leaves with almost neon green tips that bend upward and deep red, magenta or purple stems or branches.

Flowering plants develop yellow-colored calyxes and sugar leaves before dying quickly.

It is typically treated by rinsing the roots with neutral pH water for at least a week, before gradually reintroducing the fertilizer.

Measuring PPM and EC can help you avoid nutrient burn.

BLOCKAGE OF NUTRIENTS

Nutrient blockage is caused by the build-up of nutrients around the roots of a plant or by pH imbalances and prevents the absorption of available nutrients.

Nutrient blockage leads to nutritional deficiencies which can cause yellowing of foliage, leaf tip burning, irregular leaf shape and size, and brown spots. Symptoms vary based on the nutrients your plant is missing.

It is generally treated with a rinse, pH checks, and nutrient adjustments.

EXCESS OF NUTRIENTS

Excess nutrients with chemical fertilizers and supplements can burn your plants.

The highly concentrated nature of chemical fertilizers means that novice growers can easily end up over-fertilizing their plants.

Telltale signs of excess fertilizer include dry, burnt-looking leaves with yellow or brown discoloration, burnt edges, and tips bent upward.

Often, novice growers end up buying other supplements in an attempt to remedy existing nutritional problems, however this makes matters worse.

Excess fertilizer must be resolved quickly with a root rinse, pH stabilization and a new fertilization program.

NUTRITIONAL DEFICIENCY

Nutritional deficiency can be caused by insufficient nutrition or nutrient blockage.

Deficiencies in nitrogen, phosphorus, potassium, or secondary nutrients can cause symptoms such as dry foliage, yellow or brown leaves, and discolored stems.

Nutritional deficiencies are cured by increasing / introducing nutrients or, in the case of nutrient blockage, solving the blockage problem first.

ORGANIC VS CHEMICAL FERTILIZER FOR CANNABIS

At RQS we always encourage the use of organic nutrients over chemical fertilizers. Unlike synthetic ones, biological nutrients are released into the soil and absorbed by plants at a slower rate, dramatically reducing the chance of nutrient burn or other feeding problems.

Biological nutrients also benefit the soil itself, supporting the development of a rich ecosystem of microorganisms that protect and work together with your plants. Additionally, the organic soil improves over time, making it ideal for outdoor growers. The fact that organic nutrients do not produce toxic runoff also reduces the impact of your crop on the environment.

While we are all in favor of organic products, we understand that chemical fertilizers also have their pros. First, they are absorbed much faster, which means they are better for situations where efficiency is key (for example in treating a deficiency).

The fact that synthetic fertilizers are made accurately to establish specific nutrient ratios also means having greater control over what plants "eat" and in what doses.

With the right genetics, enough nutrients, water and lots of light, you'll be well on your way to growing some great weed. Remember: The biggest weapon in your arsenal is experience, so keep hone your skills and reap your rewards.

Chapter 24 Drying the Plants

After months of endless waiting, harvest time has finally come, even if you already feel like you can savor the smells and flavors of your tasty flowers. It is in moments like these that you have to keep calm and above all pay the utmost attention to what you are going to do, considering that even a single and simple mistake could throw away all these months of hard work. And we are absolutely sure that this will not be the scenario you want!

So, once the marijuana buds are harvested, you need to arm yourself with a little more patience and work on that substance, knowing that the freshly picked buds are not yet ready for consumption, because they are still too fresh. The buds of marijuana in these conditions could in fact contain substances that would make the consumption very unpleasant, but above all they would not give the desired effects. But how to intervene, then?

It is quite simple: it becomes necessary to act with cannabis drying.

Let's go in order!

At the time of harvest, the cannabis inflorescences still contain all those substances essential for their survival, such as chlorophyll, sugars and starches, which need to be eliminated to ensure a product that is tasty and healthy for consumption.

Chlorophyll, for example, is active as long as the plant is alive, but if it is not dried once trimming is done, then this substance remains in the flowers, giving it a bitter and unpleasant taste. Furthermore, a fresh bud always has the risk of becoming moldy, and as we know mold is made of highly contaminating spores, which could compromise all the other inflorescences.

Finally, it is always good to remember that in some ways marijuana drying is like putting a wine in a barrel: it is aged to make it of better quality, thus giving it time to be able to develop its aromas and active ingredients to the maximum.

The good reasons for which the famous "cannabis drying" process must be carried out have been explained, so now we can focus on another fundamental point of our research: the two phases of hemp drying.

All experienced growers are aware of this detail, but it often escapes newbies.

First, you need to keep in mind that the final cannabis treatment is divided into two stages: the drying of the actual hemp and the curing period. The difference between the two is clear, since in the first phase the freshly cut buds will be placed in a dryer with a low level of humidity, while during the tanning period the flowers must be placed inside specific containers, in the dark and with a humidity of 62%. The timing is also different, as are the conditions of the environment in which they are treated. If these two steps are successfully passed, then the cannabis drying will be complete and the product ready for consumption.

First of all, it is necessary to explain where it is more appropriate to dry our buds, and only then how to do it.

Unfortunately for our needs for synthesis, however, we must immediately admit that there is no single and perfect place to do it, because in reality any closed, dark and well-ventilated environment is a possible candidate for this process.

In fact, inflorescences need to lose almost all the water they contain, and to do so the environment that hosts them must certainly be not very humid, with a humidity rate of around 40-50% and a temperature between 18 and 25 degrees.

Additionally, it is recommended to make the environment as dark as possible, as the light could degrade the THC molecules once the buds have been harvested. Above all, it is essential to aerate the environment, which allows faster drying of cannabis and prevents the onset of mold.

To ensure efficient ventilation, for example, we can equip ourselves with a system of fans and aspirators, but it is also necessary to place the tops at a safe distance, allowing all the inflorescences to be affected by the air currents we are going to create. As for humidity control, to decrease it it is sufficient to increase the recycle of air (in some cases also of the dehumidifiers), while to increase it a humidifier or some basin of water placed on the ground in evaporation will be sufficient.

The techniques for drying marijuana

Let's now pass instead to the place and the best drying techniques. Some growers use a free growbox, as this already has the spaces set up for ventilation, humidity control and total darkness, while others, perhaps more ingenious, use wardrobes, clothes boxes or even entire rooms (in case it is an industrial type cultivation). Most of these growers also use activated carbon filters within the ventilation system, which are able to eliminate the pungent odor emanating from the buds, which becomes stronger and stronger during the process.

As for the techniques, they are mainly two: hanging the branches with the flower's upside down, or placing them inside an accordion dryer (better said: drying grids).

The first method is a favorite with outdoor growers, as the buds of these plants are much larger and take longer to dry, while the second is a favorite with indoor growers as the buds are more compact and manageable. Bud care in the first case is simply limited to respecting the aforementioned parameters, while in the second case it is necessary to turn the buds many times to prevent them from flattening, developing mold or drying unevenly.

How long does the cannabis drying process take

After explaining how to prepare for drying, let's now talk about the timing of this process, influenced by several factors. Usually, the duration is around 7 to 14 days, but it all depends on the size of the buds and how you carried out the trimming.

The thicker the buds, the greater the amount of water they have to lose, and therefore the longer the waiting times will be. It is no coincidence that the smaller buds will already be ready after a few days, while for the larger ones we should wait longer.

As for trimming, it is certainly advisable to do it when the plants have consumed all the water in the substrate, so that they are less humid. Finally, remember that the drying environment is crucial, so if you respect the rules set out above, you will be able to contract more drying times.

But how do we know that the cannabis drying period is over and we can move on to tanning? It is the buds themselves that make us understand.

First of all, they will turn out to be shrunken (since they have lost water), and - moreover - they will give us a joint signal with the elasticity of the branches. Just take a line for the branch and try to bend it: if it breaks immediately then it is ready, if it is still flexible, we will have to wait a little longer.

We also remember that drying the buds too quickly inevitably leads to a poorer product, with a too herbaceous and bitter taste. In fact, in this way the inflorescences do not have the time to evaporate all those substances such as chlorophyll and starches that make it fresh, but above all the conversion of THC from the acidic to the neutral and psychoactive form is not guaranteed. So, don't rush, let the marijuana drying take its course, and you will see that the final result will be much better.

After the cannabis drying period, we can proceed with the tanning, which requires less space than the previous one, but more constant care. To tan the buds, it is necessary to place them in dark airtight containers (but in the absence of them you can easily opt for the wide mouth glass jars). It will be sufficient to fill them for 3/4, thus leaving space for the circulation of air and thus avoiding the appearance of mold. After filling the containers, they must be stored in a cool, dark and dry place.

Once the above has been done, it will be necessary to check the inflorescences every day for the first two weeks, with the inspection that will be carried out on each bud, since some could develop mold and therefore also infect all the others.

Furthermore, it is a good idea to leave the containers open for at least 5-10 minutes a day to allow the air to be exchanged, and continue like this for at least 14 days. After about two weeks the ganja should be ready to smoke, but ... we recommend that you be even more patient. Recalling once again the comparison with wine, in fact, it can be remembered that even cannabis becomes stronger and better if it is aged properly. A 4–6-week tanning should already be enough to reach the maximum potential of your buds, but some more experienced consumers even reach a tanning period of over 6 months.

And once the tanning is finished too? The preservation of your ganja is always similar to a tanning, but this time you must not overdo it with the recycling of air, otherwise you could risk making the product too dry and crumbly.

If you plan to keep your inflorescences for a long time, we advise you to opt for vacuum containers, inside which it is advisable to insert humidifying bags, which keep the internal humidity at 62% (a percentage also useful for the tanning period). Finally, remember that even the surrounding temperature is important, and must not exceed 25 degrees, otherwise your buds may dry out too quickly.

Returning to the subject of vacuum jars, remember that it is essential that these are opaque or that they manage to protect the buds from direct sunlight. In fact, the sun's rays tend to degrade the THC molecules, thus making our product poorer and less effective. It should also be noted that there are currently many containers on the market for the tanning or preservation of your marijuana. Once you put your herb inside the jar, you will have to close it with the lid by pressing a button, which will release all the air in the container, thus making the internal environment vacuum and odorless. But if you want something more low cost, then you can always opt for a glass turntable with a rubber seal closure, which will allow you to have a watertight container.

Also, in this case we can choose the format that is most useful to us, but remember that these jars are transparent, so it would be better to find a way to opacify them. Finally, if you are growing in secret or just want to hide your weed from unwanted eyes, you can always choose the purchase of stealth containers. These products always have the appearance and shape of objects of common and daily use, such as combs, toilet brushes, screws, etc., but inside them there are always secret compartments and invisible compartments that will make your stash impossible to find.

We conclude this chapter with a warning about a very common mistake, which is mostly made by newbies. Obviously, during all these processes the buds must be handled, but you have to do it with care and the minimum necessary (we recommend the use of gloves if you are in contact with possible bacteria, fungi or even if you are heavy cigarette smokers). In fact, the heads of the trichomes, ie where the active ingredients that give us the "hit" are stored, are very sensitive, and their breaking could compromise the effectiveness of the product at the time of consumption.

Chapter 25 The Enemies Of Cannabis Plants

Cannabis is not immune to diseases or parasites. Beginners often find it difficult to spot problems such as nutrient deficiencies, pests, mold or watering errors, and are therefore handicapped. This guide will help you recognize the symptoms of the most common ailments that plague cannabis and get healthy, productive plants.

Like any other plant, cannabis can also be attacked by parasites, fungal infections, viruses and various other problems that can compromise the quality and quantity of the final crop. Knowing how to distinguish a nutrient deficiency from mold or root rot, for example, is essential to promptly and effectively treat the problem afflicting the plant, limiting the repercussions on its health.

Too little or too much nutrients can cause stress in cannabis plants, which may exhibit symptoms such as discoloration, leaf malformation, or slowed growth. Some of the nutrient-related cannabis problems include:

Nutritional deficiencies

Less experienced growers often believe that cannabis only needs three elements: nitrogen (N), phosphorus (P) and potassium (K). These macronutrients are certainly important for healthy and vigorous development. However, to complete the vegetative phase and start flowering, cannabis plants need a varied mix of macro and micro nutrients, as well as secondary substances. When specimens do not receive the right amount of nutrition, they exhibit deficiencies that can cause leaves, both young and old, to die and discolour.

Nutrient deficiencies are generally caused by inadequate nutrient delivery, pH imbalances and nutrient absorption problems. If action is not taken promptly, a nutrient deficiency can hinder the growth of the plant, reducing the quality and quantity of the final yield.

Symptoms of a nutrient deficiency vary according to the substance present in insufficient quantity. Some of the most common symptoms are:

- Death of young or old leaves
- Yellowing of the leaves
- Red or purple stems
- Dry or blotchy leaves
- Curved edges or tips of leaves
- Vertical growth
- Deformed leaves and stems

Some nutritional deficiencies can be solved by simply increasing the dose of nutrition administered to the specimens. In case of pH imbalance, and / or lack of absorption of nutrients, the plants must be subjected to different treatments.

Nutrient burn

Nutrient burn is the exact opposite of a deficiency. In fact, it occurs when plants receive a greater amount of nutrition than normal needs. Over-feeding of nutrients is the main cause of a nutrient burn, but this problem can also occur if there is a pH imbalance or nutrient block. Typical signs of a nutrient burn are dryness and yellowing of the leaves and sometimes curvature of the edges and tips.

When administering nutrients, it is important to follow a regular schedule, and check pH and electrical conductivity levels before and after each administration. In this way you will have the certainty that the specimens are receiving and absorbing the right amount of nutrition correctly.

It should be noted that nutrient burn is usually associated with the use of chemical fertilizers. Natural substances, characterized by a gradual release formula, generally do not cause nutrient burns, as they are broken down and absorbed more slowly by plants.

Nutrient Block

Nutrient blockage is caused by a chemical reaction between the plant, the substrate and the fertilizer. This reaction prevents the specimen from absorbing nutrients from the substrate and consequently leads to a nutrient deficiency.

Nutrient block usually occurs when concentrated chemical fertilizers are given for an extended period of time. Small amounts of salts and other elements present in the fertilizer can accumulate in the substrate, alter the pH levels and interfere with the absorption capacity of the plant.

Typically, nutrient block is resolved by rinsing the substrate with pH balanced water and restoring the usual feeding regimen. Many growers choose to reduce the amount of nutrition given to avoid running into the same problem again.

Cannabis Problems Related to pH

Unlike other plants, cannabis can only absorb nutrients within a narrow pH range. If the soil, water or fertilizer do not fall within these parameters, the plant will not be able to assimilate the nutrition adequately. There is therefore a risk of wasting expensive nutrients, and food deficiencies and / or absorption blocks may also emerge.

Cannabis plants prefer slightly acidic soils with pH levels of 6–7. However, we have found that slight fluctuations in pH between 6 and 7 improve the ability of cannabis to assimilate various macronutrients, micronutrients and secondary elements.

Cannabis plants grown in hydroponics or soilless grow optimally with pH levels between 5.5 and 6.5. Again, small fluctuations allow the specimens to absorb a wide range of nutrients.

Symptoms of Poor or Excess Watering in Cannabis Plants

Insufficient or excessive watering interferes with numerous physiological processes of the cannabis plant, causing stress and stunted growth. Too wet or dry soil can attract parasites such as mushroom flies, red spiders and other pathogens.

Unfortunately, a lack or excess of water causes similar symptoms on cannabis plants: the leaves begin to wilt and, over time, wither and eventually die. By testing the ground, it is possible to identify the error committed; if the soil is completely dry, it is necessary to irrigate more frequently. If it is wet and muddy, it means that too much water has been given.

To avoid too little or too much watering, remember to:

Dip a finger in the ground up to the first joint and give water only when the ground is totally dry.

Cultivate in light and airy soils, using pots with adequate drainage holes.

Perform defoliation or lollipopping on specimens to improve ventilation at ground level and allow for quick drying.

Cannabis Problems Related to the Root System

The roots keep the plant anchored to the soil, but they also absorb oxygen, water and nutrients from the substrate, carrying them to the stems, leaves and flowers. Furthermore, depending on the needs, the root system of a plant conserves and releases the energy produced during photosynthesis, to stimulate the growth of the specimen and heal any injuries.

The most common root problems with cannabis are:

Tangled Roots

Root entanglement can occur when the plant's root system is too large for the size of the container. The roots begin to grow around the circumference of the pot, forming a compact tangle. This causes stress to the plant and impairs its ability to assimilate water and nutrients. This condition can cause nutrient deficiencies, pH imbalances and blocking of absorption.

If the plant's roots are tangled, you will need to transfer the specimen to a larger container. When decanting, try to untangle the roots (where possible). In severe cases, it may be necessary to prune the roots using a pair of shears or a sharp knife. After the relocation, give the plants at least a week to recover from the stress of transplanting.

To avoid further entanglement of the roots, transfer the plants to larger containers regularly and at the appropriate time - before the roots reach the walls of the container. Seedlings, for example, can be moved into larger pots after they have grown sufficiently in height and have developed leaves that exceed the circumference of the initial container.

Root rot

As you can guess from the name, root rot is characterized by diseased and rotting roots. In substrates such as soil or coir, this condition is caused by drainage problems or excessive watering. Both factors cause an accumulation of water around the roots, favoring the proliferation of bacteria and fungi.

In hydroponic systems, root rot is caused by excessive heat, lack of adequate light, lack of oxygen in the water, or decaying organic material in the tank. All of these causes facilitate the development of bacteria and fungi (such as Fusarium) inside the tank, causing root rot. Rotten roots have a brown hue, a slimy appearance, and sometimes give off a nauseating smell. On the surface, the diseased plant appears curved and wilted, with yellow or white leaves. Root rot can also cause nutrient deficiencies, as the plant cannot absorb the elements present in the substrate.

To treat root rot, it is necessary to administer beneficial bacteria capable of counteracting pathogens. If you are growing in the ground, you can transfer the plant into a container with fresh, well-ventilated soil, checking that the container has sufficient drainage holes. If you are growing in hydroponics, however, you will need to disinfect the entire plant, create a new oxygen-rich water tank and solve problems related to heat or lack of light.

Cannabis Problems Related to the Environment

Whether you are growing indoors or outdoors, environmental factors such as temperature, humidity, light and ventilation can put stress on the plant if not properly regulated.

Heat or Frost Stress

To thrive, cannabis plants need to be exposed to specific temperatures during the various stages of their life cycle. If temperatures are too high, the leaves will tend to curl upwards, taking on a dehydrated appearance. Over time, heat stressed plants can develop white or brown spots along the edges of fan leaves.

The first step in dealing with indoor heat stress is to install fans around the plant and a ventilation system that removes stale air and replaces it with fresh air from outside. If this strategy proves insufficient, you can add an air conditioner that allows you to control the temperature inside the grow room. Finally, if your lamps give off too much heat, you may want to choose alternative lighting systems (such as LEDs, for example).

Extreme heat can damage cannabis plants, but intense cold also causes numerous problems. If the specimens are exposed to temperatures below 15 ° C, their growth may slow down (due to the reduction of photosynthesis processes). They will also be more susceptible to pathogens, such as mold. Although they show no signs of stress, plants subjected to low temperatures usually offer lower yields than those grown at optimal temperatures.

To avoid these problems:

Use a thermometer and a hygrometer to measure the temperature and humidity inside the grow room.

Use fans to allow air to circulate around the plants.

Use a ventilation system to allow air circulation in and out of the grow room.

Use LED grow lights that give off little heat.

If you are growing outdoors and facing extremely hot or cold temperatures, check the weather forecast regularly and move plants indoors in case of frost or heat waves. You can also use greenhouses to have greater control over temperatures and / or humidity levels.

Light Burn

Light burn is a problem that mostly affects inexperienced growers with limited space. It occurs when cannabis plants stay too close to the light source, resulting in bud discolouration (during flowering) and yellowing of the leaves.

Fortunately, light burn can be remedied very simply. It is in fact sufficient to remove the lamps from the plants. If this is not possible, we recommend applying techniques such as LST to induce specimens to grow predominantly horizontally rather than developing a tall, tapering structure.

If you grow outdoors, you won't have to worry about any light burns - the sun is too far away to cause severe burns to the plants. But if you grow seedlings indoors, remember to gradually expose them to sunlight so they can get used to it.

Wind Damage

Cannabis loves light breezes. However, strong winds can cause irreversible damage to plants, tear the foliage, break the branches on which the buds grow, or completely eradicate the stem.

For indoor growers, wind is usually not a problem. But when growing outdoors, it is important to take a few steps to protect the specimens:

Place cannabis plants near others or near fences, flower beds or walls that can serve as protection.

Carry out topping and training on plants. Short, thick, and compact specimens are less likely to be damaged by wind.

Grow clover around the roots of plants to prevent uprooting.

Don't overdo the support posts: plants need flexibility to be able to accommodate the wind without breaking.

Mold on Cannabis: Bud Rot and Powdery mildew

Mold is a serious problem for cannabis growers. This pathogen steals life from the plants and in some cases attacks the buds, destroying them before the grower can even harvest them. The two types of mold that afflict cannabis most frequently are powdery mildew, or sickly white, and botrytis (bud rot).

Powdery mildew manifests itself as a fine, white, flour-like powder on the surface of the leaves. Progressively, this mold spreads throughout the rest of the plant, hindering the photosynthesis process and causing the gradual yellowing of the leaves, until death. In the advanced stages, powdery mildew can deposit small black spores on the specimens, which are dispersed in the air. There is no definitive cure for healing infected plants. The only solution is to combat mold and limit its spread, while at the same time favoring the development of the unharmed parts of the plant.

Botrytis, also called bud rot or gray rot, typically nestles at the base of the stem and slowly climbs up to the branches, destroying any buds it comes in contact with. Symptoms of a botrytis infection are wilting, discoloration and dryness of the leaves on individual flowers or the entire bud. Looking at the affected parts, you will notice the presence of a gray or bluish mold. Over time, botrytis produces small black spores that can spread to other specimens by air or by direct contact.

Fighting cannabis mold is complicated. First of all it is important to identify the pathogen that has infected the plant. Later, you can decide whether to attempt to save the specimen.

A fungal infection can reduce the quality and quantity of the final crop. Unfortunately, mycoses occur quite frequently in both indoor and outdoor plantings. Therefore, prevention is key.

Damping-off or Seedling Dying

Damping-off is a common fungal infection that mainly affects young seedlings. It is generally caused by Pythium, Botrytis and Fusarium fungi (more on this below). Whether already present in the ground or transported to the grow room or garden by an infected specimen, these pathogens attack the stem of the seedlings, causing them to collapse and subsequent death within 24 hours.

Septoria

Septoria is a fungus that occurs with yellow spots on the leaves. It attacks the foliage, scattering it with yellow or brownish patches. It typically affects specimens that have just entered the flowering phase and initially appears on the lower leaves. If not treated promptly, Septoria spreads to the rest of the plant; although it doesn't usually hit the buds, it can destroy much of the foliage. This infection causes enormous stress to the plant, and also compromises its photosynthesis processes, resulting in a slowdown in development and a reduction in final yields.

Fusarium

Fusarium is a fungus capable of destroying an entire cannabis plantation. It can lie dormant in the ground for years and strike without causing any symptoms. It is therefore very difficult to detect this infection. The fungus concentrates mainly on the root system, causing rot and interrupting the distribution of nutrients and water to the entire plant. Diseased plants begin to sag and wilt, and eventually die — sometimes within a few days. There is no cure for Fusarium. Growers dealing with this infection are often advised to cut down the entire plantation, throw away soil and pots, disinfect the growing area, and start a new crop.

Pythium

Pythium is a parasitic alga, previously classified as a fungus, which attacks the roots of the cannabis plant. It is a major cause of root rot. Pythium can affect a specimen at any stage of its life cycle, but the seedlings present a higher risk due to the tendency to moist substrate.

If you are growing in hydroponics, you will be able to recognize an infection caused by Pythium more easily. The signs that indicate the presence of root rot are brown pigmentation and a slimy, slimy mass around the roots of the plant. Pythium is responsible for over 90% of root rot cases.

Unfortunately, if you grow in the ground or with passive hydroponic systems (for example coconut fiber or perlite), you will have much more difficulty in identifying the presence of Pythium, since this pathogen causes visible symptoms on the plant, but often attributable to other problems, such as deficiencies. nutrients or light burns.

Alternaria

Alternaria infections are estimated to cause the destruction of about 20% of all agricultural crops.

Alternaria proliferates in hot and humid environmental conditions. It mainly affects plants grown in poor quality soils, those that have already suffered parasitic attacks previously or specimens that do not receive adequate doses of nourishment. Alternaria can attack the plant at any stage of development, but occurs mainly on specimens in the flowering phase. One sign of Alternaria infection is yellowing of the edges and the presence of purple-brown patches on the leaves. Sometimes small dark spores also appear on the foliage (called conidia).

Unfortunately, Alternaria is not treatable. This fungus is transmitted by seed and spreads rapidly from one specimen to another, infecting the fruits and making them inedible.

Verticillum

Verticillum is another devastating fungal infection. This fungus can lie dormant in the soil for years, and then become activated and hit the root system of the plant. Verticillum then attacks the xylem — plant tissue that carries water and nutrients from the roots to the rest of the plant.

In the course of its expansion, the fungus blocks the xylem, hindering the flow of water and food, and causing necrosis and wilting in various sections of the plant (including leaves, branches and flowers). Verticillum can also cause brown pigmentation around the stem near the ground.

Like many other pests, Verticillum spreads quickly and causes serious damage to the plant. If you notice the presence of this fungus in your garden, you should remove all infected specimens and sterilize all types of equipment to avoid the proliferation of spores. To avoid the risk of future infections, it will also be necessary to remove the soil.

Viral Cannabis Problems

Unfortunately, viruses are difficult to detect, especially for less experienced growers. However, these pathogens can cause severe damage in a short amount of time.

Tobacco Mosaic Virus

First detected in tobacco plantations, the tobacco mosaic virus (TMV) causes malformations and curling of the leaves, as well as crisp yellow, mosaic-like patches. In some plants, the stem may appear faint and discolored (usually a red or purplish hue), while other specimens may harbor the virus without showing any symptoms. Although rare, tobacco mosaic virus infection is not curable. If you spot this pathogen in your garden, you will need to eliminate all infected plants to avoid the spread of the disease.

Parasites are a fairly common problem for cannabis growers, especially outdoors.

Mushroom flies

Mushroom flies are small black colored insects, very similar to fruit flies. Unlike other parasites, they do not affect either the leaves or the flowers of the plant. However, the larvae proliferate in the soil and slowly eat the roots. Over time, this infestation can cause yellowing of leaves, wilting, symptoms of nutrient deficiencies, and slowed growth.

Unfortunately, mushroom flies are a very common problem for cannabis growers. The larvae may already be present in the prepackaged soil, but excessive watering and high humidity levels can also attract these pesky insects to the garden or grow room.

Thankfully, mushroom flies aren't particularly dangerous pests. Neem oil, diatomaceous earth, and beneficial insects or bacteria (such as ladybugs and Bacillus thuringiensis) can help you keep fungus flies under control, as long as you intervene promptly on the infestation.

Red Spiders

Red spiders are very common pests that can completely destroy your plantation. These small arachnids exhibit black or red hues, and prefer warm, dry environments. Unfortunately, they reproduce very quickly (females lay up to 20 eggs per day, for 2–4 weeks), so it is essential to identify the infestation as soon as possible to minimize damage.

The first signs of the presence of red spiders are small patches or dots on the surface of the leaves and thin white cobwebs on the underside (which progressively spread over the entire plant). If nothing is done, these little creatures can kill the leaves and interrupt the development of the plant, reducing its productivity.

Red spiders are particularly resistant to most pesticides currently on the market. To treat a red spider infestation, we recommend removing the affected leaves, washing the plants with a mixture of water and neem oil and introducing ladybugs to kill these pests and prevent future attacks.

Aphids

Aphids are some of the most destructive pests for cultivated plants, including cannabis. Observed under the microscope, these insects appear as small green, black, red or white crickets or grasshoppers, ranging in size from 1 to 10mm.

Females lay eggs in early spring and the number of specimens increases rapidly within a few weeks. After entering the grow room or garden, these insects begin to feed on plants, leaving behind a soap-like substance (called honeydew) that settles on leaves, stems and flowers. Honeydew attracts ants and molds, which can damage the plant and ward off predatory insects such as ladybugs and, consequently, favor the proliferation of aphids.

In addition to destroying foliage, aphids can spread disease to other specimens. As in the case of infestations by red spiders and mushroom flies, we recommend removing the diseased leaves, cleaning the plant with a mix of water and neem oil, and introducing beneficial insects that can counteract the aphids and prevent their reappearance.

Leaf miners

Leaf miners are larvae of various insects, which - as the name suggests - tunnel into leaves to feed on them. They look like small light yellow or green worms and are about 1mm in size.

Young specimens of leaf miners take refuge in the ground during the winter and emerge in the spring. As adults, they begin to make their way to the leaves, where they deposit their eggs. The newborn offspring will feed on the leaf, until they fall into the ground and start the life cycle again.

Leaf miners create typical white or yellow lines on the leaves. As in the infections of red spiders and aphids, it is necessary to remove the affected leaves, wash the plants with water and neem oil and use predatory insects capable of eliminating leaf miners.

Caterpillars

There are over 20,000 species of caterpillars in the world, all with one thing in common: The ability to destroy a cannabis plantation.

Whether they are moth or butterfly larvae, the caterpillars will feed on your plants and may even (temporarily) dwell on them, creating cocoons in the foliage. Most caterpillars eat and lay eggs on the leaves, but the corn borer and Eurasian hemp moth dig tunnels inside the stems.

The only way to protect plants from caterpillars is to regularly inspect the specimens with a microscope or magnifying glass, and eliminate any caterpillars or eggs (which may have black, white, or red hues) present. Also check for holes in the stems and traces of brown color, symptoms of a burrowing caterpillar infestation.

Other Common Problems in Cannabis Plants

In the grow room, many other issues can arise, from revegetation to accidental pollination.

Hermaphroditism and Bananas

Cannabis is a dioecious species, meaning it produces plants with distinct male and female reproductive organs. In the case of hermaphroditism, however, both sexual organs emerge on the same specimen. This can be caused by genetic factors, seed manipulation or stress.

Hermaphroditism is the expression of a survival instinct. The production of sinsemilla (seedless) cannabis is far from natural — females are not fertilized for long periods of time in order to stimulate resin production and increase the potency and flavor of the fruit. Unfortunately, these long flowering phases (in addition to stressful environmental factors such as inadequate temperature and humidity levels, poor lighting, improper administration of nutrients and pH imbalances) can cause the female to develop male sexual organs, called "bananas", such as extreme attempt to self-pollinate.

Recognizing hermaphrodite plants is simple, as long as you know what to look for. However, you will have to identify them promptly to prevent them from fertilizing the females, ruining the entire crop.

Inversion and revegetation

A cannabis plant in the flowering stage can revert to the vegetative stage if its lighting cycle is interrupted. Beginners may accidentally reverse the plant's development cycle, but experienced growers sometimes induce revegetation on purpose to get multiple harvests from the same specimen. Although it may seem like an advantageous operation, revegetation involves some risks: in fact, regenerated plants offer lower yields and can show signs of hermaphroditism.

Pollination

Pollination is a deadly sin for anyone looking to grow sinsemilla (seedless) cannabis. After being fertilized, the females will stop producing resin, focusing their energies on creating seeds. One sign that reveals a female's pollination is the swelling of the bracts. Open a bract with the help of a pair of scissors: if you find seeds inside, your plant has been fertilized.

Unfortunately, it is not possible to reverse the pollination process. The only solution is to eliminate the males, evaluate the level of pollination of the other females and decide whether to keep or remove them too and start a new plantation.

Chapter 26   Growing Marijuana in 10 Steps

For some people, growing cannabis is a hobby. Many want to achieve self-sufficiency by growing a few marijuana plants, while others aim to become true professionals. But what really matters is the seed. In this step-by-step guide we will follow you on your first growing adventure.

GROWING MARIJUANA IS SIMPLE

Cannabis is grown all over the world by the most diverse people. Self-production is very simple and can offer excellent harvests even for those with no experience. The only things you will need are a little knowledge and enough willpower to follow the entire cultivation plan. These 10 simple steps will show you how to proceed from planting to storage in jars. Get ready to join a fast-growing community.

STEP 1: DECIDE WHETHER TO GROW INDOOR OR OUTDOOR

The first decision a grower has to make is which style to adopt. Growing outdoors is worthwhile if the weather is warm and the plants receive at least 8 hours of direct sunlight per day. The indoor, on the other hand, allows you to cultivate 365 days a year. The outdoor growing season in the warmer southern regions can range from early spring to autumn. In the colder climates of the northern regions, the best interval to grow is 8-10 weeks warmer than summer.

Timing is essential for outdoor growers. Sow too late and the first winter colds could ruin plants that are now close to harvest. Sow too early and photoperiod strains will grow in the vegetative phase for long periods of time, until the natural day-night cycle approaches 12 hours of light and 12 hours of dark, triggering flowering. Indoor growers, on the other hand, have total control over the light cycles.

SUNLIGHT

Outdoor growers need to sow at the right time. To understand this, you need to check the weather data and climate forecasts available for your location. Another important factor to consider is whether to use pots or plant directly in the soil. Cannabis plants need strong sunlight. If you plant in pots, you will be able to move the plants more easily to sunnier areas, in case the shaded areas increase as the season progresses. Also, if the weather gets worse, you can repair the plants indoors.

TRADITIONAL LAMPS FOR GROWING

For indoor growers, a lighting kit and timer are essential. HID lamps are a reliable and reasonably priced light source. The 400W and 600W dimmable digital power supplies are a great choice if you are planning a grow on a budget. You can place an extractor at the height of the reflector to bring the lamp closer to the plants and reduce excess heat (and keep electricity bills under control). Micro-growers who use small closets or closets should settle for a 250W lighting system.

Both MH lamps for vegetative growth and HPS lamps for flowering become hot. The air intake and exhaust fans must be powerful enough to maintain optimal environmental conditions. When growing with multiple lamps, air conditioning may be required. The three main parts that make up a traditional lighting system are the power supply, the lamp and the reflector, still widely used by growers today.

Step 2 MOST ADVANCED LIGHTING TECHNOLOGIES

CFL bulbs are more suitable as supplementary lights during flowering or as the sole source of light during the vegetative phase, as an alternative to MH lamps. They don't get hot, but their light doesn't penetrate like that emitted by HID or LED lamps. They can be kept very close to the top parts to limit energy consumption.

LED lights are the lighting technology for the indoor grower of the future, already available today. Unfortunately, the best LED kits are expensive, but the Full Spectrum ones can be used for the entire life cycle of cannabis plants and are ready to use right away. This next generation lighting system does not require ballasts, reflectors or lamps to be replaced every year.

Among their main advantages, LED lights do not overheat and, compared to HID lamps, they emit much lighter than heat. If you are planning on growing cannabis for long periods of time, investing in a high-quality LED kit will save you a lot of money. The latest generation LED kits have a life expectancy of around ten years and consume 50-75% less energy than HID lamps. In the long run, LED lights will save you money on your electricity bill.

STEP 3: SUBSTRATE

Cannabis plants can grow in the most diverse substrates. The three most used are soil, coir and substrates for hydroponics, such as expanded clay. The earth is the most forgiving and acts as a buffer for the root zones. Coir and substrates for hydroponics, on the other hand, require greater precision in fertilizing. Beginner growers prefer to grow in soil for this very reason.

However, starting a crop in coconut or hydroponics is not difficult at all. On the other hand, you have to start somewhere. The main difference is that soil normally contains enough nutrients to support plant development in the first few weeks of growth, while coconut and hydroponic crops require fertilizer from the start.

Always buy cannabis-specific substrates in grow shops. Universal slow-release soils from garden centers are not suitable for growing cannabis. It takes a lot of experience and practice to design a custom "super-soil". Until you gain enough experience in growing cannabis, rely on substrates sold in grow shops. They are quite cheap and avoid unpleasant surprises.

STEP 4: FERTILIZATION

Cannabis-specific fertilizers are essential. In most grow shops you will find packs specially designed to offer all the nutrients for plant growth. They can be found in different brands, with lines tailored to meet the needs of the substrate of your choice. Some fertilizers are already formulated with optimal pH. For novice growers, correcting the pH with each watering may be just another cause for concern.

If, on the other hand, you are using a line of fertilizers with a suboptimal pH you will have to monitor the pH levels of the substrate, raising and lowering its levels until you reach the perfect range. To do this you will need a pen pH meter and a bottle of solution to lower or raise the pH. Those who grow in soil must maintain a pH close to 6.0-6.5, while in hydroponic and coconut crops the pH must be kept at 5.5-6.0 to optimize the absorption of nutrients.

In general, chemical fertilizers are better suited for hydroponics as they create less salt build-up which could block irrigation systems. Organic fertilizers, on the other hand, are perfect for soil crops. With coconut fiber, an additional supply of calcium and magnesium may be required.

Beginner growers should avoid supplements and enhancers and only use basic fertilizers. Magical potions and wonderful elixirs can only be a waste of money in these first steps in the growing career. We rather recommend a simple fertilization plan, consisting of macro and micronutrients to be alternated with water only. Silicon is often overlooked, but it should be made as an essential weekly supplement for all substrates.

STEP 5: CHOOSE THE SEEDS WITH CRITERIA

Genetics will be the deciding factor in all cannabis crops, both indoors and outdoors. The best strain will obviously be the marijuana most dear to you. But it must also have the most appropriate dimensions for your spaces.

Indica-dominant hybrids and autoflowering strains are generally easier for beginners to grow. They require no special care, stretch less and complete the cycle faster, especially compared to the taller and later sativa-dominant strains. Bending and pruning are techniques that require some skill and experience to master. If this is the first time you are growing, avoid complicating your life and only grow low and bushy plants, rather than tall and slender. Wanting it all too soon can be counterproductive.

STEP 6: GERMINATE THE SEEDS

There are several methods of germinating seeds. However, since you are new to the world of cultivation, the simplest method with the highest success rate will suffice.

And if you decide to grow outdoors, then we recommend that you germinate the seeds indoors first. Many growers leave them on a sunny windowsill throughout the seedling stage before transplanting them into the great outdoors. Daytime temperatures should be between 20 and 30 ° C, without dropping below 15 ° C at night. This is the optimal temperature range for most cannabis plants.

STEP 7: VEGETATIVE PHASE

As soon as they emerge from the substrate, the young seedlings require light. You can transplant them from the Smart Start to the final pots as soon as they reach 2-3cm in height. Photoperiod cannabis strains can stay in vegetative growth indefinitely as long as an 18/6 light cycle is maintained, but will normally transition to flowering after 4-8 weeks. Outdoor growers should start in the spring / summer when the days are longer.

Autoflowering strains are characterized by vegetative growth phases of 3-6 weeks and start flowering regardless of the light cycle. These varieties can also be sown out of season, with excellent results. Hybrids with ruderalis genetics require at least 18 hours of light for their entire life cycle, which can last from 8 to 12 weeks. In their early stages of development, cannabis plants do not require large amounts of fertilizers and supplements. A supply of nitrogen fertilizers and enzymes will be sufficient for root development.

Cannabis plants also give off very pungent aromas. If you are growing indoors, you should invest in odor control devices. Install an activated carbon filter on the air extractor with devices to channel and / or diffuse the absorbed odors around the plants.

STEP 8: FLOWERING

Indoor-grown photoperiod strains go into the flowering phase when they receive a 12-12 light cycle. The flowering phase can take 8 to 12 weeks. The light-dark cycle must be homogeneous and uninterrupted. Outdoors, cannabis flowers naturally and gradually as the days get shorter in late summer / early fall. As previously mentioned, autoflowering cannabis instead starts flowering regardless of the light cycle.

Nutritional needs shift from nitrogen to phosphorus and potassium. Nitrogen fertilization is reduced and buds require more P and K. Many growers also bring bloom boosters at this stage. There are cannabis strains that can double or triple the heights during flowering. In indoor crops the heights of the lamps will have to be adjusted several times to avoid burning the tips of the inflorescences.

STEP 9: HARVEST

In the last or penultimate week of flowering it is necessary to carry out a thorough washing of the growing substrate with water only or with a solution for "flushing". Fertilizers spoil the flavors when you skip this step. Organic fertilizers also need to be washed off.

You can use the stage of development of bud hairs to determine the best time to harvest the plants. When 50-75% of the pistils have taken on a reddish, orange, pink or brown color, the flowers will be ripe. For greater accuracy you can use a pocket microscope to observe the head of the trichomes. When most are milky in color and some tending to amber then you can harvest. If they were still transparent, it would be better to wait.

To harvest the plants, you can cut branch by branch or the entire plant at the base of the main stem. At this point you will need to remove most of the leaves around the flowers. The resin-coated leaves can be set aside to make hash. Put on a pair of latex gloves and use handy manicure shears for the buds to get the best clean up.

STEP 10 DRYING & TANNING

Freshly harvested buds cleaned of leaves should be left to dry in the dark for 10-14 days, at room temperature and 50% relative humidity, ideal for avoiding mold. Some growers hang buds on a string inside closets, while others prefer to remove as many twigs as possible and place them on nets, moving them daily to even out drying. Popcorn tops can be dried in brown paper bags for about a week.

You are obviously free to smoke a few days dried marijuana, but if you want to savor all its power, flavors and fragrances you will also have to cure it. By simply storing the inflorescences for another 2-3 weeks in the dark and inside glass jars you will be able to cure your marijuana.

The ideal would be to maintain a relative humidity of 60%, opening the jars for 10 minutes every day, to prevent any accumulation of moisture. If you are patient you can savor all the cannabinoid content and the aromatic profile of the plant.

Chapter 27 The Laws On Cannabis Use Around The World

The term marijuana indicates a substance that is obtained from the seeds, leaves and dried flowers of Indian hemp. You may have heard of it in street jargon where it is also known as cane, cannon, joint, joint or many other more or less funny names.

Marijuana is a hallucinogen and is therefore considered a drug. The debate on its use has always been very heated. It must be said that the consumption of the substance for medical purposes is now cleared of customs in many parts of the world: marijuana is in fact useful in the treatment of some diseases, especially degenerative ones of the nervous system.

We leave judgments on the legitimacy of its use to you, and if you are willing to share this dream state that marijuana promises to induce, here is a map of the places where it is legal to consume it.

States where it is legal or substantially legal

There are some states in the world where using cannabis is legal, tolerated or allowed but with some restrictions. In the US, some states have enacted laws to regularize their use, especially for medical purposes.

There are other realities where the consumption of marijuana is entirely allowed, indeed it is part of the traditions of the country.

Five states in the US: Colorado, Washington, Alaska, Oregon and the District of Columbia. Average cost: $ 11 per gram

Uruguay, but consumers are forced to sign up for a special register. Average cost: $ 1 per gram

Netherlands, not legal but tolerated for sale in Coffee Shops. Average cost: $ 30 per gram

Bangladesh, where there is no law in this regard and is therefore, in fact, totally legal. Average cost: $ 0.50 per gram

States where it is illegal but decriminalized

If the list of countries where the use of marijuana is legal is really small, a little more substantial is that of the states where it is illegal but by penalized. By decriminalization we mean that consumption for recreational purposes and, above all, the sale or sale, remains prohibited.

The permitted actions, on the other hand, are the production and sale by specialized companies, and consumption for medical purposes, prescribed by a specialist. Furthermore, the penalty for possession does not include imprisonment.

Spain, possession and consumption not in public places is legal. Average cost: $ 10 per gram

Portugal, the sale is prohibited but, since 2001, possession is legal. Average cost: $ 5 per gram

Italy, decriminalized personal consumption and allowed medical use, but it remains illegal. Average cost: $ 10 per gram

Switzerland, the consumption of hemp by adults is punished with a fine of 100 francs. Possession of less than 10 grams is not punishable. Average cost: $ 10 per gram

Austria, decriminalized personal use of a modest amount, allowed cultivation for therapeutic use. Average cost: $ 11 per gram

Czech Republic, no sale, allowed possession of up to 15 grams of marijuana and cultivation for personal use. Average cost: $ 11 per gram

Germany, possession within 10 grams is not prohibited, use is legal. Average cost: $ 10 per gram

Australia remains illegal in some states but decriminalized in others, legal for therapeutic use. Average cost: $ 15 per gram

Argentina, legal only to possess up to 5 grams for private use. Average cost: $ 5 per gram

Chile, the laws in force do not punish personal and private consumption but sanction group consumption. Average cost: $ 5 per gram

Paraguay decriminalized possession from 1988 up to 10 grams. Average cost: $ 3 per gram

Peru, possession for personal use of up to 8 grams is not illegal, but about 60% of inmates are in prison for crimes related to mere detention. Average cost: $ 10 per gram

Colombia allowed possession up to 20 grams, legal medical consumption. Average cost: $ 10 per gram

Ecuador decriminalized personal use. Average cost: $ 10 per gram

Costa Rica, consumption and personal possession do not represent a criminal offense. Average cost: $ 20 per gram

Jamaica, possession (up to 56.70 grams) and decriminalized use since 2015, allowed the cultivation of up to 5 plants. Rastafarians can consume it in places of worship. Average cost: $ 10 per gram

States where it is illegal but often not prosecuted

In these countries the use of marijuana is pro the scope and pursued at the legislative level, but at the same time more or less widely tolerated.

Mexico is illegal but some people have obtained special government clearance for cultivation and lawful consumption for recreational purposes. Average cost: $ 15 per gram

Brazil, clear distinction between traffickers and consumers, the crime is decriminalized. Average cost: $ 10 per gram

India, use is permitted for religious purposes. Average cost: $ 3 per gram

Cambodia, police are not stopping consumers. Average cost: $ 3 per gram

States where it is completely illegal

In the rest of the world, the use of marijuana is still illegal and its use is a criminal offense. However, the punishments for this type of crime vary greatly from state to state, ranging from simple fines to prison, up to corporal punishment.

Marijuana is prohibited in a large part of Europe, in the whole of the African continent and in almost all countries of the Americas and Asia.

Croatia, the possession of even just one gram severely punished with a fine, risks from 3 to 15 years in prison for cultivation and sale

Romania, fines for the possession of small quantities, the sale and possession of large quantities provide for imprisonment

Belgium, completely illegal in any form

France, illegal, up to one year in prison

Japan, since 1948 all preparations containing THC are illegal

Israel, illegal, allowed medical use only if authorized by the health ministry which evaluates it on a case-by-case basis

New Zealand, illegal

Poland, illegal in any form, with sentences ranging from 3 to 10 years in prison

UK, illegal

Other states of which there is no information

North Korea, it is unclear whether the possession, consumption and production of this substance is legal or not. Some sources claim that the law does not prohibit the use, others warn tourists of cannabis that North Korea is not a paradise but actually spinels, being discovered in posses s or the substance can lead to serious legal consequences.